WHEN WORDS COLLIDE

SouthWest Manuscripters

ANTHOLOGY

First printing: February 2013

Book cover design by Jay Simpson

ISBN: 978-0-9890146-0-1

E---mail: SWMtws@hotmail.com
Website: http://www.coliserv.net
Blog: http://southwest-manuscripters.blogspot.com
Also: http://southwestmanuscripters.wordpress.com

ACKNOWLEDGEMENTS

Thanks to my wonderful anthology committee members Vickey Kalambakal, Barbra and Jay Simpson, Connie Bessman Natt, Janis Lukstein, Bernadette Shih, Beth and William Wittenbury, our historian Ian "Van" Gordon and our copy editor Professor Dan Lambert, Niki B. Burgi, designer, and Tibor Polgar, consultant. Their support as team players helped me to stay focused and kept me in track with the project despite my grueling schedule. I pledged to pull this project off in 6 months...and here we are! Congratulations to all of you, SWM members who contributed to this historical book through your talents and creativity.

But foremost, thanks for our prominent member of over 50 years, our beloved mentor and friend, the late Ray Bradbury who generously shared with us his knowledge, his passion to write and his love for life and people. He encouraged us to reach our fullest potential through his invaluable insights.

Ray Bradbury's memory shall live on through all of us and continue to be an inspiration and role model of excellence.

Ildy Lee
President 2012
Executive Editor and Project Director

Ray Bradbury *Ildy Lee*

TABLE OF CONTENT:

Barbra Holt Simpson

Born and raised in Russell, Kansas, Barbra received a Bachelor of Fine Arts degree in Painting and Printmaking at the University of Kansas, where she met and married her husband, Jay, a graphic designer. Barbra completed a Master of Fine Arts Degree at Wichita State University.

She moved from the plains to California, became a Realtor at the beach, and continued writing through UCLA Extension classes. She studied poetry with Myra Cohn Livingston and Laurel Ann Bogen.

Barbra is compiling a chapbook of poems in memory of their beloved son, Steven, who passed away from complications of Multiple Myeloma. She has completed illustrations for a book of poetry and songs written for her grandson, Beau Stephen Simpson, with plans to self publish both books.

Snow Mass placed 68th in the 80th Annual Writers Digest Writing Competition. *A Holding Time,* Third Place winner, published in the 2012 Writers' Digest 7th Annual Poetry Collection, is not in this SWM Anthology.

E-mail: *barbra_holt_simpson@aol.com*

BLUE

The boy skipped flat stones
into the dust of a water-well blasted
to nowhere, rocks piled against
the burning wind. Wind slapped
his denim overalls and white shirt
to his bones. Devils of dirt
swirled in the bald, red soil.

Daily, the old Cherokee checked his oil,
Wells --fresh drilled black scars--
on deeded tribal land.

Sunlight burnished his buckskin pony
like a promise. The greyhound, scrawny
and sleek, loped behind, or raced
ahead in a rolling rhythm of turns
creasing the dust as she chased
rabbits that veered into her beat,

Head down, ears back, the dog
raced toward the boy,
nosed his crotch and pocket
where he kept his lucky rabbit's foot
and sprinted away.

The boy whistled until his lips
cracked thin
on onion flake skin.

Once, the boy glimpsed the Indian
and ran after the horse,
through a sticker patch
of goat-head thorns
stabbing his feet.

Although he never saw
the greyhound again,
he remembered her
and watched for her.
Throwing his pocketknife
into a sand hill of red ants,
the boy heard hoof beats
and squinted
into the noonday sun.
Purple mesas shimmered
on the horizon
or was it a mirage?

The Indian leaned from the saddle,
holding a squirming, blue-brindled,
greyhound pup. The pup nuzzled
the boy's ear, snuffled
his hair, licked tears
from his cheeks.

"Blue," said the boy.
"I'll name her Blue."

TANGLED WEBS

Caught in branches and crotches
Like small kites,
Pouches of twigs and silk
Woven like knitted gloves
With fingers bared,
Embalm the trees.

Climbing like blossoms
Of the night blooming moon-
flower,
Cream-colored webs
Entomb
the larval moth--
Multitudes of future
generations.

Encased within her silken
And translucent shroud--
Her abdomen filled with
larvae--
The mated pairs embrace
Like captive lovers, knowing
Only one will survive.

THE SITE

Disturbed, the earth gives up her dead.
Buried shards and bones are restless
Beneath the leaves,
Revealing privileged secrets.

BEAR

A Peanut Butter Bear
left his lair
in the spring
And promptly ate
all the food
that I could bring
He liked especially
sweet honey,
and his peanut butter
runny,
Then climbed up
my
tree
for a swing.

FOX

The fox is both
Charming and sly,
  Lives a life
Secluded and shy.

He sat there watching, paying no mind,
   When a big fat chicken
   Walked up from behind.
Now he sleeps in his den,
Had for breakfast that noisy hen,
For his dinner, a chicken pot pie.

Quicker than a blink of your eye.

ELEPHANT

A baby
elephant
has to learn
to drink
and
dunk
with
his trunk.

He drinks water
with his nose,
holds it tightly
closed
and plays
and sprays
like a hose!

SPIRIT VOICE:
THE DIRECTIONS

North: *Season of the Cold Moon*

Black hair braided long, doe-
skin dress as pale as mountain snow
beaded in porcupine quills and turquoise sky,
I rest on a smooth white rock, cry
and hold my belly.
Two ermine drink fully
from a trickle of snow melt.
I trap one sleek winter pelt
to hang upon my low-slung belt.
My spouse runs to catch her mate.
He will take that prize
for his warrior's shield.

I race over drifted hills and field,
and win. Pains begin.
His son, stillborn
"Did you not know these
were always yours?"

He caresses ermine skins.
I cradle empty moccasins.

South: *Season of Long Days*

I ride a Pinto, follow
tribal elders through a dry arroyo
to canyons where weathered petroglyphs
are chipped and incised on limestone cliffs.

The People, hundreds traveling
this path before,
have forgotten these stories—
our ancestral lore.
I chant and sing the language
the ancients shared
Medicine Woman raises her arms
in prayer.
Spirit animals are with me:
Black Wolf, a shadow I cannot see,
but hear a growl and know
he is near,
Puma screams in warning not in fear,
Eagle circles overhead
To point the direction where I am led.

East: *Season of Little Leaves*

Medicine Woman invites me
to sit in ancient ceremony.
I do not know this rite:
I pass the basket on
full of strawberries, ripe,
and passed to me again,
the last one, I touch to my lips.
Sweet red juice drips
freely on my tongue.
"Did you not know, these
were always yours?"
Medicine Woman blends with the wind
to join the old women
holding the horizon.

West: *Season of Falling Leaves*

Fine red grit blinds my eyes,
sifts into my nose and throat, dries
my skin, tough as hide.
In this windswept space, I decide
to place small moccasins and deer
skin dress, the color of ochre,
and bury beneath the crumbling ruin
Two yellowed skins of ermine.

On this barren mesa near the skies,
Black Wolf's yellow eyes
One last time stare into mine.

Puma leaps onto the craggy incline.
The seasons of our days are done.
We soar with Eagle to meet the sun.

PRAIRIE SEASONING

Kansas in June, heat
hangs in sunlit sheets.
LeRoy and me shed our clothes
at the creek
belly deep, switching gnats,
mud squished between our toes,
snorting cool water like cattle,
bare-handing catfish--
our hands bloodied by spikey fins--
butts sunburned, that last summer
before we went to war.

SNOW MASS

Why now do I dream
of snow melting, running swift
in icy streams,
a knife, undercutting sleeping drifts?

I have been away – gathering time
in years of summers, awakening
to relentless surf as sand sharks swirl
shallow in ochre tinted water,
scuttling through clouds
of their own making.

While speckled brook trout,
illusive within the suns
reflected sheaves
of darting brilliance,
lie invisible in clear shadows,
waiting, suspended
between heaven and earth.

Illustrations by Barbra Holt Simpson

Bernadette Shih

Bernadette Shih was born in China and emigrated to the United States as a young girl. She continued her education in the United States gaining a BA in East Asian Studies from the University of Washington and an MA in Library and Information Science on a Harvard University Internship Program.

Bernadette has devoted much of her working life to bridging the cultural divide between her old home of China and her new, Western world through the medium of literature. She has held the post of Chinese Literature Specialist at the Massachusetts Institute of Technology Libraries and headed the National Science Foundation project for that library in conjunction with the Yenching Library of Harvard University.

Bernadette is the author of *Becoming American,* a collection of short stories on acculturation. Her other publications include two volumes of poetry, *Song of Life* and *Love: Leap of the Heart and a Sweet Tear;* two popular children's books: *Ling Ling: The Most Beautiful Giant Panda in the World* and *Good Friends;* and a biography of Mao Zedong, *Mao—A Young Man from the Yangtze Valley.*

A member of the Authors Guild, The Academy of American Poets, The American Association of University Women, PEN USA, and the International Society of Poets, Bernadette lives with her husband William on the beautiful Palos Verdes Peninsula in Southern California.

AT THE GATE OF PARADISE

Seasons come and go
Soon autumn will be upon us

Memories
veiled by mist and lingering clouds
causing bitter tears to run down
my shivering cheeks

In my garden of summer splendor
early autumn wind whistles sadly
sink deep into the abyss of my being

Like dust
I am blown about in all directions
swinging between dreams and illusions

Sorrows come
Memories weigh me down

A lost bird
I long for my own forest of eternal joy
Choked by reverie
I ache for lost moments forever gone

Am I condemned
to a life of wandering alone in darkness
infinity touches the edge of my yearning heart

Will glimmer of light fall upon my wretched paths
and I would wait not forever
at the gate of paradise

Beth Eichel

Beth Eichel, former national president of National Charity League, Inc., is definitely a California woman. However, much of her current writing is about growing up in Oklahoma. In addition to the CDs *Windowsill of Heaven, I'm A Country Girl in a City Woman,* and *Women of Spirit,* two of Beth's musicals have been produced. *Porches* was written with Dr. Louise Midget, and *Skating Cracked Sidewalks* is a one-woman show. Beth continues to speak to groups and share her music. Visit her website at: *www.betheichelproductions.com.*

"You will laugh. You may cry. You will be touched, and maybe even inspired. And you'll most definitely be entertained..."

-- *Palos Verdes News* on her one-woman show, *Skating Cracked Sidewalks*

BARKLEY THE DOG

A story in rhyme

There once was a puppy named Barkley, the dog.
He wasn't a pig and he wasn't a hog.
He wasn't a goat and he wasn't a cat, but
To tell you the truth, he didn't know that
'Cause when he woke up, he was all alone
And he didn't know if he was full grown!

But, before I go on, I must tell you this,
Barkley, the dog, could only say, "Hiss."
He couldn't bark, and he couldn't growl.
He couldn't whine, and he couldn't howl!

He didn't know this, and he didn't know that...until
He met a kitten named Pat.

Now, Pat was very wise for her age.
She had read all the library books page by page.
Most of her time was spent in a book, but
Every day she walked by a brook, and
She knew this and she knew that!
She was very wise, this kitten named Pat.

One nice day, Pat was walking along,
Whistling a tune and purring her song
Until she heard a "Hiss" by the path.
When she saw the puppy, she started to laugh!

"Only snakes hiss!" she said to the pup
Who was so embarrassed, he couldn't look up.
He hung his head down and it got so low,
That it pulled him over and Pat said. "Oh, no!
I am so sorry. Are you all right? And
Barkley, the dog, said, "Hiss" out of fright, 'cause

He didn't know this and he didn't know that
Until he met a kitten named Pat.

"Oh, I feel so bad! Your feelings are hurt,"
Said the kitten named Pat to the pup in the dirt.
"I am so sorry! That was so mean!
Sometimes my mouth just becomes a machine
And the words that I speak are those of a rat!
Please, do forgive me. My name is Pat."

So, Barkley got up and he "hissed" his name
And the kitten named Pat began to explain that
They could be friends. She could help him a lot.
And she asked the dog if he could foxtrot.
And the puppy named Barkley gave her a nice "Hiss"
And the Kitten named Pat purred and gave him a kiss.

They purred and they hissed as they danced to the brook
And they purred and they hissed through the rest of this book.

And every day, the pup met the cat
And she talked about this and he "hissed" about that and
Pat taught Barkley all that she knew and
Barkley taught Pat a fine thing or two.

And Pat kept on reading and she learned to be kind
To animals, children and people she'd find
And Barkley discovered that he was a pup
And "hissing" was super ok growing up, 'cause
Who needs to bark or to growl or to talk
When "hissing" communicates all of that squawk!

So, Barkley grew into the nicest old dog
And he became friends with a pig or a hog
And a goat and a horse and a frog named Jose
They made doggone music in every which way!

Some would sing that and others sang this
As Pat would purr and Barkley would "hiss."
And every new voice improved on the song
And all of God's creatures loved getting along.

The path to the brook was the happiest place, 'cause
They all got along in the animal race!

Beth Whittenbury

Beth likes to inspire with her writings and hopes you will enjoy her two entries in this anthology. A lawyer by training and a mother in practice, she writes on a wide range of subjects.

She has written and published two law-related, non-fiction books, along with numerous related articles in both peer reviewed law journals and trade magazines.

Beth also writes legal thrillers, commercial non-fiction, picture books, and screenplays. Please catch some of her writings on her website, *www.HouseSpouseChatter.com*, where you can post your own prose on the "Writing" page. Her commentary can be viewed at *bethwhittenbury.wordpress.com* and *hsccollegetestingtips.wordpress.com* as well. Please free to read and post your own comments on either site.

JUST LOVE HIM I GUESS

When I first saw him, I had to smile.
A cuter baby hadn't come in a while.
We named him William; we cuddled; he'd coo,
But we still didn't know just what to do.

He weighed in at six pounds, nine ounces.
His neck was so fragile, he couldn't take bounces.
He didn't know how to eat or drink.
When put in the car seat, he seemed to shrink.

He couldn't walk; he couldn't talk,
So when he would cry, I didn't know why.
"What am I going to do with you?" I asked in despair.
"Just love you, I guess. I really do care!"

William grew and although his teeth came through,
He couldn't quite chew.
That motion was strange. He didn't understand.
Teeth are to chew food, not gnaw on your hand.

Mush didn't seem fun, so new food we would try
Spaghetti was next but, oh no! It doesn't fly!
William thought it more fun to throw than to eat.
Big globs of spaghetti soon landed at Mom's feet.

"Please stop that," she asked, and pleaded and cried,
But William threw farther each time he would try.
"What am I going to do with you?" Mommy was mad.
She looked at the red-stained face of her dear little lad.

"Just love you, I guess." There are worse things you could do.
Little did she know that prediction soon would come true.
The love got us through.
Then, William was two.

William wasn't bad as little boys go
But sadly, he learned to use the word "no."
He loved his baths so much, he wouldn't get out
Mommy would say, "All done," and William would pout.

"What am I going to do with you? The water is cold!"
"Just love you I guess, but you're much too bold!"

Soon William made friends who were pretty good kids.
Except for the time they cut up the tuna can lids.
"Those are sharp and dangerous, didn't you know?"
William said, "Oh Mom, just go with the flow."

"I love you honey, I must keep you from harm."
"Hey, stay away from those bees, they're starting to swarm!"
It's hard to raise children to be fearless and true,
When most of their games really scare you.

"You must stay where I can see you and use common sense.
"Young man, come back here. You can't climb that fence!"
"What am I going to do with you?" I'd say in dismay
"Just love you I guess." That will work for today.

One of William's favorite things was building forts.
To him, it was much better than playing most sports.
He built one at school with sticks and some grass.
He recruited some friends to help after class.

To hold it together they needed concrete.
So, they mixed mud with water. Oh, what a treat!
For a mixing container, he looked all around
Then used his back pack he had set on the ground.

When Mom saw that, she was quite upset.
The backpack was ruined and all sopping wet!
"What am I going to do with you?" she asked very loud.
"Just love you, I guess," but she wasn't quite proud.

Now William's Dad loves to make model planes.
When crafting them by hand, he takes great pains.
To William they looked just like fun little toys,
And using them in play battles brought him great joy.

He got them down from high on a shelf,
And zoomed them and zagged them just like an elf.
When two collided in a great dog fight,
They sadly could no longer take flight.

When Daddy found out, he began to shake.
William was so scared, he began to quake.
"What am I going to do with you?" Daddy spewed.
Then he looked at William's little face, and his love renewed.

"Just love you I guess," he said with a sigh.
He put the planes back together hoping they'd still fly.

One day William decided to make Mom and Dad breakfast in bed
He wanted them to feel loved, happy, and well fed.
So, he climbed on the counter to get them a dish
But then getting down became his only true wish.

He called for help, woke his folks with a start.
They ran to help, tripping over his play cart.
On the counter they found him with dish in hand
As he teetered there, they wondered what he'd planned.

"What are we going to do with you? We both just ran!"
Then, they looked around and understood his sweet plan.
The little guy smiled, and his parents did too.
"Just love you, I guess, and we both really do."

Then, one day, William took out all his toys.
He started to build with them: one of his joys.
He built part of the fort before school time came.
To his parents, the room looked a mess they could hardly contain.

While he was at school they put the toys away.
They thought that by cleaning for him,
He'd have more time to play.
When William came home and found his fort gone,
He got really mad, and he felt like a pawn.

He shouted, "What am I going to do with you?"
Then, he stopped and remembered just what to do.
"Just love you, I guess," he said with a smile.
The hugs they all shared went on for a while.

INSPIRATIONS FROM THE SEA

When my soul cries for uplift and my prayers need a boost, I go to a special place that never ceases to inspire me. Close to my home, a dirt path snakes along the bluffs which line the ocean in a wriggly crescent known as Golden Cove. Sometimes I let the strains of beautiful music blend with the sight of the waves as I trundle along the trail. Other times, so deep run my prayers that I hear only God's voice directing me on to better life works.

Today as I travel my special road, I see an anomaly in an otherwise placid sea. The unusual sight stops me and pulls me to the railing as I strain to understand the mysterious sight before me. The otherwise calm water appears disturbed in one place where a significant bow wave moves across the water. I see no vessel or anything on top of the sea to cause such an irregularity.

I frown, actually concerned for the ocean's lack of placidity, wondering what evil forces disturb the otherwise smooth, glistening water. Then I begin to understand. A school of dolphins joyfully swim together at full speed, jumping and frolicking to such an extent that they stir the ocean and push the water ahead of them to form the significant wave steadily passing across my gaze.

I smile as I realize my inspiration. What can appear to us as a disturbance in life can, in fact, arise from forces of good working together toward a common goal. We must look beneath the surface and not let our limited first view of a situation block our recognition of the good actually going on underneath. If our life seems caught in a violent tempest, throwing us into whirlpools of worry, perhaps such apparent tumult really works to propel us onward in the proper direction - toward a destination we don't even know awaits.

So, I stop worrying and lift my thought up to see where I'm impelled to go next. My day begins, and I'm off on a new, productive adventure. Next time you see the ocean, stop and see what lessons it teaches you.

Beverly Knudson

Beverly was born into a large extended family of Slovenian ancestry in Cleveland, Ohio. Introduced to dance at the age of six, she did acrobatics, ballet and excelled in tap dancing. She moved to the San Fernando Valley with her parents and sister at age ten. The balmy weather of Southern California agreed with her health and she changed from a short skinny girl to a tall girl of normal weight. She attended Van Nuys High School with celebrities and children of parents in the entertainment industry. Dancing took a back seat when she became interested in sports. After attending Valley Community College for two years, she attended the Dental School of the University of Southern California. Shortly after graduation she married an aerospace engineer and they produced three sons. Her career in Dental Hygiene was a joy and she was a part time clinical instructor at her alma mater for five years. She is now retired and enjoys her family, friends, writing, singing, playing bridge, gardening, and community volunteer work.

IMMIGRANTS

A chapter from "The Linden Tree Legacy" by Beverly Knudson

Late in the afternoon on the first day of May in 1924, sixteen-year- old Josip knocked on Anton Poncek's door. A man, near to his age, opened the door and said, "Hi. Who are you?"

"I'm Josip, Frank Koznar's son."

"Great! We've been waiting for you. Ma told me you'd be staying with us for a few months. Come on in. We'll have to find you a place to sleep. There's no regular bed for you."

Josip stepped into the parlor and said, "Don't worry. I sleep anywhere. What's your name?"

"I'm Ivan, Anton's son."

Josip was standing on a large fringed carpet covering a shiny wood floor. A small piano stood in the corner in front of lace-curtained windows. The cozy room was spotless and Josip felt good being there. This was a wealthy family, at least wealthier than his family. He was puzzled by a piece of furniture that had a tenor voice singing from it.

"That's Enrico Caruso. His voice is playing on a phonograph record on a machine called a Victrola. Ma loves opera. The family bought the Victrola for her birthday. Josip's here," Ivan shouted toward the back of the house.

A middle-aged woman wearing slippers and a print dress covered with an apron, stepped into the parlor. In English, laden with a Slovenian accent, she said, "Welcome. How are you today?"

Josip responded, "I'm fine and glad to be here."

"This is my Ma. Her name is Louiza." Ivan said.

They heard Caruso hitting a high note.

Louiza asked, "Do you like opera? Hmm, maybe you haven't heard opera before."

"I don't think so. My Mom has a wonderful soprano voice and sings a lot." Josip said.

"You must be hungry. Ivan will keep you company while I finish making dinner," Louiza said.

"C'mon, let me show you around," Ivan said.

Ivan took Josip into the dining room and showed him an adjacent small room next to a flight of stairs, saying it was his uncle's bedroom. The tiny room had a separate bathroom next to it.

"I never saw an indoor toilet before," Josip said.

"It was a very old house when we bought it. We modernized it and added a second floor."

They climbed the stairs to the floor above, where there were three small bedrooms. Ivan pointed to each room. "My three sisters sleep in that one. My parents sleep in that one and my brother and I sleep in this one. I'll ask Ma for extra blankets so you can sleep on the floor next to us. Now I'll show you the gazebo Pa and I built," Ivan said.

They went down the stairs, through the dining room and into the kitchen where Louiza was putting noodles in a large pot of soup. An attractive young woman was cutting cabbage on the kitchen table. Ivan introduced her, "This is my oldest sister Theresa, named after our grandmother."

Theresa looked at Josip with big brown eyes and they stared at each other for a few seconds before she said, "Hi."

Josip responded, "Hello." No other words came to him.

The two young men bounded out the back door of the kitchen and into the side yard where a newly painted gazebo gleamed in the fading sunlight. The two-toned green structure had a swing inside.

Ivan explained with enthusiasm, "Pa wanted his gazebo to be the best in the neighborhood, so it has eight sides instead of six. We drew the plans last summer and finished constructing it before the first snow fell. The two-by-four pieces of lumber support each side to gives it strength. The wainscoting is two-and-a-half feet from the floor and the lattice walls let the breezes flow through. The raised brick floor and roof sheeting makes it leak-proof. The thick chains attached to the swing make it quite sturdy. See the soldier at the top of the roof?"

A little wooden soldier was mounted on the roof peak and painted to look like a military officer. He had a black fez cap, a red jacket with yellow buttons, blue pants, and black boots that reached to the knee. For his arms, he had propellers attached from shoulder to shoulder by a steel rod. When the wind moved the propellers, the soldier whirled around, changed directions, stood still, and spun again.

"We bought the wood soldier from a neighbor and replaced the arms with propellers. Theresa copied a picture of a Turkish military uniform, when she painted him. The neighborhood kids like to watch our soldier perform. Once, someone tried to steal our soldier. We found gouge marks in the wood platform he's standing on and a hammer lying next to him. We think the thief had difficulty loosening him without damage and gave up. The soldier is securely anchored so a strong wind won't blow him away."

"Did you ever find out who did it?" Josip asked.

"No. Pa thought the culprit was one of my friends." Ivan said.

"Do you think I could sleep in the gazebo when the weather gets warmer?" Josip asked.

"Sure. I think it will be okay." Ivan said.

They returned to the house through the kitchen. Louiza was mixing the soup.

"Can I do something to help you?" Josip asked.

Ne, ne, ne (No.) Sit down and I'll get you some wine," Louiza said.

Josip sipped the red wine slowly as he watched Theresa move about the kitchen. The back door opened and a middle-aged man entered.

"Anton this is Josip, Frank's son," Louiza said.

Anton said hello in Slovenian, "Zdravo," and then sat down at the kitchen table and poured himself a jigger of schnapps. After swallowing all of it at once, he drank a glass of beer. Then he said, "How is your family?"

"Mom and Dad aren't well, but my brother and sisters are fine," Josip said.

"I'm sorry to hear that about your parents," Anton said.

Josip told Anton about his siblings and the health problem his father was having due to mining bituminous coal.

"Ya, that's a very hard job your Dad has," Anton remarked.

At 6 p.m. the family gathered in the dining room and Ivan introduced Josip to the rest of the family: Uncle Boris and his two youngest sisters. Anton sat down at the head of the table and Ivan sat on his right. Josip was motioned to sit beside Anton and the family sat in the remaining chairs. Louiza and Theresa placed bowls of food in front of Anton and sat at the other end of the table. Before anyone lifted a fork, Anton's deep voice thanked the Lord for all his blessings. His speech slurred by the boilermakers he drank. Anton took the first scoop of soup and then helped himself to the meat, potatoes and slaw. After taking a share of the food, Ivan passed the bowls to Josip, who passed them on to Boris.

It was obvious Ivan was the oldest by the way his siblings spoke to him. Anton's half-brother Boris, did not resemble Anton at all because he was shy, small of stature and stuttered. Theresa was quiet compared to her younger sisters, who laughed and chattered constantly. Halfway through the meal, Anton admonished them and they quieted. Josip thought the whole family was handsome, except for Boris.

The children spoke fluent English while Louiza and Anton struggled with their new language. By watching Anton and Louisa listen to their children converse in English, Josip suspected they understood the language better than they could speak it. The family talked about their schools, jobs and neighbors. They did not hide their feelings; laughing or showing sorrow at the slightest provocation. Dinner was over when Anton got up from his chair. The men meandered away while the women cleared the table.

The women sang while they washed the dishes and Anton and Boris played cards in the kitchen Ivan, Stefan and Josip sat in the parlor and talked.

"I need to find work, do you know anyone that would hire me?" asked Josip.

"Let me think. Hmm, we have a friend that owns a machine shop. He always needs workers. Get a pencil and paper and I'll give you the address," Ivan said.

"Thanks. I'll go there first thing in the morning," Joseph said.

There was a light knock on the front door. Ivan opened the door and greeted the woman standing on the step. "Look who's here. It's our favorite cousin Fritzy."

A rotund woman with a sweaty face came into the room and said, "Dober vecer," (Good Evening).

Just then, Louiza came into the parlor to hug and greet her cousin. Everybody was somebody's relative or neighbor in the small Slovenian community. Louiza pointed to Josip and said,

"This is Anton's dear friend's son and he's going to stay with us for a while."

Fritzy hugged Josip. Her body odor repulsed him and the shrillness of her laughter hurt his ears. He retreated from her, making sure he kept his distance.

Stefan whispered in Josip's ear. "Fritzy has some kind of disease. Her smell has something to do with her illness."

Ivan said, "Nice to see you Fritzy," as he retreated to his room with a book in hand.

After chatting with Fritzy for what seemed like an eternity, Louiza yawned and said "Lahko noc," (Good night).

Fritzy smiled, showing her yellow crooked teeth, and said, "I'll come back tomorrow. Adijo."

As the door closed behind the family cousin, Stefan remarked, Fritzy is really nice and gives us things she knits."

"Yeah, but I have to stand away from her, I have a sensitive nose," Josip said.

"You'll get used to her. She has no husband or children and she comes here almost every day. I'm going to bed. See you upstairs," Stefan said.

Joseph's attempt to sleep on the floor of the brothers' bedroom was futile, even though Louiza had provided him with a soft pillow and a comforter. Stefan and Ivan wrestled in bed, pulled the covers off of each other and made a lot of noise. After an hour of trying to sleep, Josip snuck down stairs with his bedding and slept on the parlor sofa. He woke before anyone else, gulped down a breakfast of bread and butter and went to the address of the machine shop. He said Ivan sent him and the owner smiled and said he knew Ivan and his family very well. Josip was nervous answering the owner's questions and thrilled when offered a job as an apprentice. Of course, he accepted.

As the weeks went by, Josip learned to become a machinist and listened to the Poncek's arguing. Coming from a more harmonious family, Josip was dismayed at the argumentative behavior of the siblings. It always seemed that one of them was mad at someone or something. He got used to Fritzy for everyone liked her and she always brought gifts she knitted herself. She gave Josip a scarf and he held his breath when he hugged her in appreciation.

Josip told Ivan about his fondness for the Pennsylvania woods. On a warm and humid day in July, Ivan asked him, "Do you want to come with me to a small forest not far from here?"

"What a great idea," Josip said.

Josip loved being in the woods again. Ivan pointed out the different trees, insects, and birds. Ivan loved the woods too and the young men bonded while strolling along the paths of the old forest. They were both the oldest sons of Slovene immigrant parents, spoke two languages, were opposite in temperament and had many siblings; resulting in a close kinship.

Stefan, Ivan's younger brother by a year, was as handsome as Ivan, but not as serious. He admired Ivan and wanted to do whatever he did and wanted whatever he had. Always vying for attention, he asked Ivan many questions and backed off when Ivan became irritated. He had a nice voice, played the accordion and was the leader of a polka band. He was not a bookworm like Ivan, who did not try to please anyone except his mother. Stefan often played the accordion after supper and the family gathered and sang songs with him. It was a happy time for them, when their voices blended in harmony.

Josip liked watching Theresa lose some of her reserve while singing and swaying to the beat of the music. He talked to Theresa every time he had a chance, trying to cheer her with a joke to elicit a smile. At first, she looked at him with suspicion and walked away. Not deterred, he succeeded in getting her mouth to turn up at the corners. Then after a few more days of jesting, she actually laughed.

One evening after supper, Josip asked Stefan about the sizable scar on his arm. Stefan answered, "Ivan liked Pa's scar so much he decided to give me one too."

"What did Ivan do to you?" Josip asked.

"The accident happened when Ivan started first grade. I was five and not in school yet so I waited for him for hours to return so we could play. When he came home, I hid behind the kitchen door and watched him eat a piece of bread while standing in front of the stove looking out the window. I jumped on his back to surprise him and he twisted me off, causing my arm to fall into a pot of water boiling on the stove. I screamed. Ma heard my cry, ran into the kitchen and wrapped a wet cloth around my arm."

Stefan continued, "We lived in an upstairs apartment then and didn't have a telephone. Ma carried me downstairs and asked a neighbor to call Pa at work. He came home as fast as he could and took me to a local doctor who said the burn was so severe, he would have to cut my arm off. 'No cut, No cut,' Pa said. He rushed me to another doctor who also said the arm had to come off. Again, Pa said, 'no cut, no cut.' This doctor told us about a medic who just returned from the war in Europe. He saved many soldiers' arms and legs by using Silver Nitrate. The burn hurt so much, I cried constantly and Pa was getting panicky. He rushed me to the third office and the medic said he could try to save my arm. He calmed me and treated me with the Silver Nitrate. The burning sensation lessened and I stopped my crying.

Josip's eyes watered, remembering his poor sister Christina and the pot of boiling water that killed her at the tender age of two. Relating the story of his sister was on the tip of his tongue, but he didn't trust his emotions, so he said, "Wow, how lucky that you found that Medic."

"That's for sure. Ma blamed Ivan for my burn and was furious with him. She chased him all over the house with a switch. He wedged himself under the stairs where she couldn't get to him and waited for her to cool off. After a couple of hours, Ivan emerged, explaining to Ma, that my arm fell into the boiling water by accident and felt sorry for me. Ivan is Ma's favorite and he wasn't punished. "

Stefan continued, "For a week, the medic came every day to treat my arm with Silver Nitrate. On one visit he brought a German helmet he got in the war and let me wear it while he treated my burn. It was a funny green color and had a leather strap. I asked him to tell me about the war. He said it was terrible and didn't say anything else about it. My arm gradually healed and the medic was happy with the result of his treatment. The last time he came, he invited me to visit him at his office. I never did.

"Now both you and your father have scars on your arms," Josip said.

Pa doesn't like to talk about his scar. All he says is that he got it from an accident when he was in the Austrian Army.

"Did you ever see the young medic again?" Josip asked. Stefan cleared his throat. "Our family went to his funeral about a year later. Ma always prays for his soul."

sIvan was munching on a piece of strudel when he came into the parlor. Ivan interrupted, "I heard what you were talking about. The medic was a swell guy. It's too bad he caught that deadly flu. In the last year of W.W.I in 1918, a flu epidemic spread throughout Europe and the United States affecting large numbers of people, including the soldiers fighting in the war. In fact, more soldiers, (called doughboys,) died from the flu than from fighting in the war. Some believe the doughboys brought the disease to the United States when they returned from Europe. This plague spread all over the world and one million people of the twenty million that were infected, died. Did the people in your town suffer with it?" Ivan asked Josip.

"I remember several of the villagers with the flu being isolated from the rest of us. This was a wise precaution because the disease didn't spread like it did in other towns." Josip said.

Ivan continued with his reservoir of information. "When the flu hit Cleveland, many people got sick with fevers, sore throats, and some died. Our young medic caught the virus while treating infected people. I think our family avoided catching the flu by Ma hanging garlic around our necks. She made us stink so much the virus wouldn't get near us." They all laughed.

THE LINDEN TREE LEGACY

BY

B.F. KNUDSON

Beverly Shue

Beverly Woo-Shue spent fifteen years working in a family Chinese restaurant while in school at 42nd Street, Audubon Jr. and Dorsey High. Dr. Bergquist majored in Bacteriology; Beverly attended UCLA and completed a BA in "Bac-T." Her secondary teaching credential enabled her to teach at a high school or community college; careers deemed desirable for women in the 1960s. Beverly holds an MA in Microbiology from UCLA.

On UCLA: "I survived and prevailed as a commuter student and learned how thick my skin is. Lack of funds forced me to find carpools everyday. Thanks to Mme Lenard for her diligence and to my English teacher for re-reviewing my Subject-A essay—it should have been given a "Pass" grade. Dr. Ruth Ball encouraged me to earn a master's degree. Gratitude to UCLA when it elected me to Sigma Xi and Phi Beta Kappa, where I earned Highest Honors at graduation."

On A Career: "I taught one year at Lincoln High School and 43 years at LA Harbor College. My service included Senate President at Harbor, District Senate President, and the Executive Committee of the Academic Senate for California Community Colleges."

CAMPING IN TOTAL DARKNESS

Spring Break, 1986—We were on Vacation and decided to drive our pickup truck-camper to the redwood forest. Shannon was eight and half, and Shaun recently celebrated his sixth birthday. Gene drove the camper, and I served as navigator, cook and dishwasher. After years of camping in cab-over campers where the roof leaked, and having to buy a block of ice every two days, we bought a Lance camper! I bought this beauty from a private party for one-half off the original selling price. What luxury! It was equipped with a shower, electric refrigerator, toilet, stove, heater and a queen-sized bed. What a contrast to our first camper: homemade and slapped together, with a roof that leaked when it rained.

Our destination was Henry Cowell Redwood State Park in Felton, California, but we stopped in San Luis Obispo for lunch at the Apple Farm Restaurant. Our real goal was to see if Mackintosh was still around. He was the Apple Farm "mascot," an overfed, orange cat. A sign read, "Mackintosh is fed on a regular schedule—Please refrain from feeding him." Based on his weight of over twenty pounds, the sign was ignored. He loved syrupy attention, but when he had enough, this orange bundle of fur walked away as tourists tried to snap one more picture.

Feed the truck was our last job before heading off for Felton. I had flashbacks to the early 1970s when Gene and I, before we had kids, ran out of gasoline while traversing the "Lower 48 states." He ignored a gasoline station's warning sign, "Last chance for the next 100 miles." We had to flag down an Auto Club truck on the highway in Cheyenne and buy five gallons of gas. When we bucked headwinds in Oregon, our truck barely made it to the gas station by coasting down the off-ramp! I vowed we would never repeat driving the camper on fumes, now that we had to protect Shannon and Shaun. We headed for Highway 101 to begin our camping trip.

The kids climbed up on to the queen-sized bed, gazed out the front window and drifted off to sleep. Light gray clouds gathered, but only moderate rain was predicted. The clouds thickened and turned darker gray. We left Highway 101 and headed toward Henry Cowell State Park I spied the "Campground Ahead" sign; Gene turned and paid our fee, while I asked the ranger, "Will it rain tonight?"

"They expect showers during the night" was his answer.

Hunting for the right camping spot meant being close to the restrooms and water, but not too close in case there were noisy campers. We parked two rows from the restroom in an isolated spot that was an easy walk to the water faucet. Shannon and Shaun explored the campground. They checked out our picnic table and fire pit, while I cooked dinner. I made hamburgers and hot soup, and we ate on paper plates, making cleanup easy. Washing the frying pan was a snap—boil some water, swish with soap and rinse. I cleaned up while everyone else slept.

The sound of rain on the camper intensified. Raindrops pelted the vent over the queen-sized bed. The pounding noise increased, and the raindrops bounced off the camper truck hood. Shannon, Shaun and Gene were sound asleep. Black clouds closed down the sky. I lost sight of the light that illuminated the restroom front doors. With rain pouring down, the angry sky crackled and lit up the campground. I counted six seconds between lightning bolts and when thunder roared. The lightning and thunder were unleashing their fury a mile away. After the lightning flashed, the campground became ominously dark. But, each time new lightning bolts crackled and displayed their jagged beauty, I could see the trees, camp tables and fire pits.

The time between lightning strikes and the sound of thunder gradually increased to eleven seconds—the angry storm was moving away and was located more than two miles from us. It began pouring sheets of rain. When I peaked out the kitchen window, I could not see our fire pit or camp table, just total black outside. No stars twinkled when I glanced up—all I saw was a pitch-black sky! Fear and tension gripped me during these spells of total darkness between lightning strikes. When the lightning subsided, rain unleashed on the camper. I could not see anything inside the camper, so I quickly turned on the kitchen lamp—I needed to see some light to calm me down. Shannon and Shaun slept through nature's light show, thunder and downpour. My panic seemed to correlate with being in total darkness. I woke up Gene and asked him to move the camper and park anywhere where I could see the restroom light from the front cabover window. The distant light calmed me down.

I mulled over how fear set in after lightning bolts stopped. Thunder didn't bother me, but sitting in a pitch-black camper without stray light from stars or even a small restroom light gripped me with fear. I felt stress when the camper darkened after the lightning stopped and relaxed when lightning again lit up the sky. This was my "Ah-ha! Moment" when I realized I was afraid of the dark! Why?

I thought about the origins of my fear. The roots were planted decades ago as a child growing up in the 1940s. My two older brothers, Tommy and Charlie, and older sister Barbara loved to play tricks on me. Their favorite prank was to hide and "scare Beverly" by screaming and jumping out at me. Tommy tormented me by saying, "Watch out for the Boogie man at night." The boogie man was a bad person who hid in dark closets.

My fears of the dark continued with the movie *The Cat and the Canary*—it showed a black cat near a spooky mansion. Creepy things happened inside. The curtains billowed as wind rushed through the windows. We saw movie characters hide in secret passages and jump out of dark closets. I was only two and could not speak English, so I had no idea of fear, other than watching my family react in horror to scenes in the movie. We walked home when it was night. I pictured dark shadows everywhere and imagined boogie men hiding behind the bushes and on every dark porch. We rushed to get through the front door. Our first task was turn on all the lights in the house, check the closets and look under the table. My crib was in Pop and Mama's bedroom. Tommy, Charlie and Barbara slept in makeshift beds Pop made by draping sheets over poles. The sheets looked like the billowing curtains in *The Cat and Canary* movie.

Pop worked in Chinatown and returned home after 2 a.m. I jumped into bed with Mama and quickly fell asleep. The movie scared all four of us, but I felt safe snuggled up with Mama. Something spooked Tommy, Charlie and Barbara around midnight. They screamed and ran into the bedroom where Mama and I were sound asleep. In no time at all, I felt the crush of three siblings on top of me in this double bed. I was pinned down under the blanket—it was stifling hot. I cried and complained, "I can't move!" Mama scolded Tommy, Charlie and Barbara. They squabbled over who was at fault for the commotion. Finally, Mama laid down the law and proclaimed, "Everyone take one corner of the bed, and I will sleep in the middle."

I buried my fear of the dark once I started first grade in Leimert Park. Class mates didn't talk about the "boogie man." I spoke English and understood the movie dialogue at the Leimert Theatre. Even the "scariest" movie in grammar school, *The Thing*, made my school friends and me laugh. Visits to "houses of horror" where ghosts and thugs jumped out of dark rooms and coffins didn't scare me—I knew these were fake and designed to frighten. Besides, the stray light in these horror houses meant it was never totally dark.

When touring Mammoth Cave in the 1970s, Gene and I carried flashlights. At a strategic location the ranger flipped off the cave illumination and asked tourists to turn off their flashlights. This allowed our eyes to adjust to the total darkness in the cave. As the ranger briefly explained the size and geology of Mammoth Cave, a few tourists mumbled about how uneasy they felt in the dark. Before the ranger concluded his talk, he told us, "I'm going to light a candle." I was amazed how much of the cave showed up. We could see the walls and geological features like stalactites and stalagmites more than 200 feet away!

I shifted from the distant past to my new epiphany, when I realized I was afraid of total darkness. This 1986 camping trip uncovered my fears (total absence of light) and defined my comfort zones (presence of at least some stray light). I'm okay as long as I can see some light, whether from stars, distant city lights, moonlight or a campfire. Today, I carry a flashlight on my key chain—I'm ready for any electrical blackout and plan to avoid ever being in total darkness. Achluophobia will never plague me in the future!

KINDERGARTEN CRISIS

I squeezed mama's index finger, not knowing if I wanted to let go and run the other way or continue being dragged toward the door. Other moms guided their children toward the rug, gave a kiss and left. Most were brave, but a few cried softly. Mama smiled and told me in *sze yup* Cantonese to follow the other children. I tried but was nervous my first day at 42nd Street School. Fear swept over me—I knew just a few words in English, magnifying my anxiety. It hit me, "I am all alone without anyone to help me out." Our teacher smiled, but her words did not register. When the class stood up. I said to myself in *sze yup*, "What does teacher want me to do?" I burst into tears when I could not explain my dilemma. I uttered, *"Gnoy em sak nay gong mut!" (I don't know what you are saying!)* The teacher sent a note to the principal asking how to handle this confused Chinese child. The principal sent a monitor to the 4th grade class, asking my sister Barbara to calm me down. She explained in *sze yup* what the teacher wanted me to do; I relaxed as I wiped away my tears. My heart stopped pounding, for now.

New apprehensions occurred over which bathrooms to use. Here were these tiny toilets, cute and just my size. What was all this *"wonk, wonk"* that fell on my ears? My screams sent a monitor to the principal—my sister came and explained, *"Nuu-doy yung cuh-goy thu-saaw"* (*Girls use this toilet*—she pointed to where the girls "go potty"). Barbara advised, "Watch the other children and do what they do!" We sat on the rug, and the piano spoke, *"Plink-plunk, plink-plunk."* The room quieted down, and all I heard was, *"Wonk-wonk"*; many *"wonk-wonks."* The children understood, "Stand up, hold hands, etc." Next came, "Tip-toe this way while I play the piano (teacher waved her hand to let us know which way to prance)." These "Wonk-wonks" made no sense to me. I repeated my *sze yup* phrase when I was confused, *"Gnoy em sak nay gong mutt!" ("Stand up! Hold hands! Form a circle! Tip-toe!")* At first I watched but did not move. I imitated the children putting arms out to the side, pretending I had airplane "wings." I checked to the front and back of me as I tip-toed around the room. Tears, the hardship of serving lunch customers and picking me up from school proved too much for Pop. Since I dreaded school, my parents withdrew me from kindergarten. I was a dropout! A school failure at age five!

After graduating from UCLA, I thought about my shaky start and asked, "Why did I fail?" I could not speak English when we moved to Leimert Park. We went from an "open, unrestricted community" near Chinatown to a restricted community governed by real estate covenants designed to exclude minorities. The bombing of Pearl Harbor changed our destiny.

Pop purchased a Chinese restaurant business from a Japanese family forced to sell after President Roosevelt issued Executive Order 9066, relocating citizens of Japanese ancestry 100 miles from the Pacific Coast. We ran Canton Café and moved into the back house. Minorities could not *rent a house* in Leimert Park but could *rent a business.* We rented a café at 4321 Crenshaw Blvd. and lived *behind* the business—this was technically OK.

The rental and sale of homes were governed by covenants, binding legal obligations written into property deeds. Examples of restrictive covenants read, "No property shall at any time be sold, conveyed, rented or leased, to any person(s) not of the White or Caucasian race." Some stated, "No persons not of the White race shall be permitted to occupy any portion of said lot or buildings, except a domestic servant employed by a White occupant of such building." A few were worded, "No person of the Negroid or Mongoloid race may remain in said buildings for more than 12 hours except as a day employee of said owner." Our family and the prior Japanese restaurant owner lived in the back storage house for a total of 25 years.

"How did restrictive covenants affect me as a child?" I was an isolated dot of yellow in a sea of white dots. I was the only kindergarten child who looked different. Most girls had light brown hair styled in curls. Mama braided my hair into two pigtails—no girls in my class had black hair or wore braids. My sister was the only other exception at 42nd Street School.

Finally, one could ask, did siblings Tommy, Charlie and Barbara suffer school shock in Leimert Park? "No," they spoke English at 28th Street School, where savvy Chinese children explained new words for children who needed help. No children could help me in *sze yup* at 42nd Street School. I was linguistically isolated, and Barbara had to rescue me when I panicked.

Dropping out of school, gave me time to explore businesses near Canton Café. Pop told me, "Avoid Wally's Liquor Store, but Wing's Chinese Hand Laundry was okay." I watched them iron and fold shirts. Dillon's Barber Shop and Mrs. Lindberg's Beauty Salon cut and swept up a lot of hair that fell on the floor. The two pet stores and Toth Camera Shop displayed glitzy goods geared for the affluent. An empty space became the first Mexican Restaurant in Leimert Park. Pop warned me of bad people and evils at the bar and cocktail lounge. Norris and Eileen Bakko's Antique Shop was my favorite—this is where Leanna and I became good friends.

I always stopped to watch the gas station with their gravity-fed pumps. The attendant fill a glass bowl to the number of gallons requested. After gasoline was pumped into a glass cone, the nozzle was depressed and gas dropped into the car's gas tank. The last business before vacant lots at Vernon Avenue and Crenshaw Blvd. was the Leimert Bowl. All tasks were done manually, from sweeping and stacking bowling pins to returning balls. When bowlers finished their games, they paid at the desk and tipped the pin boys by sliding coins the length of the alley. Some businesses complained when I played on the front sidewalk, so Pop told me to stay out of sight. He preached, "Idle hands are the workshop of the devil." Translation: "You're not in school, so it's time to learn restaurant work." My first jobs were safe, dusting the booths, sweeping the floor and washing the kitchen counters. I learned to peel snow peas and shrimp, and wash celery and *bok toy.* I read the Herald Express newspaper three times each day.

In the Fall of 1944, first grade started at 9 a.m., while fifth grade started at 8:20 a.m. My siblings walked to school at 7:30 a.m. I stayed behind and said nothing when Pop did not drive me to school. My "dreams" of never going to school were dashed when the front opened and a man entered, asking for Mr. and Mrs. Woo. The truant officer warned, "You must send your daughter to school—it's the law." My carefree days came to a stop. Beverly the kindergarten drop out had no choice. No more loafing and lazing through the day. My twelve-year journey of attending school began the next day. I did not cry or pout, because it was harder to entertain myself during the day. My ears tuned into English, and I learned to greet customers. Being small for my age meant the ladies gushed, "What a cute little child!" I just loved this attention.

I needed time to adjust to school, and I was relaxed because I finally understood English. I still remember the first sentence I uttered in first grade: "The sky is blue!"

Bonnie Folkart

A resident of the South Bay since 1949, Bonnie was an RN for 24 years after which she returned to school to obtain a MA in Clinical Psychology. For the last 32 years she has been a California licensed Psychotherapist with a local private practice.

In addition to Southwest Manuscripters, Bonnie is also a member of the Southern California Haiku Study Group.

SANE PARENTING WITH TEENAGERS

(or "Some ideas to avoid inheriting insanity from your teens")

Suggestion #1: Fill a glass with your favorite beverage and toast the discovery of the Cat Scan (CT). Recent studies have shown that teen brains light up very closely to schizophrenics. Not exactly, but very, very close.

#2: Do not expect to carry on a rational conversation with your teenager. Ever tried to have a rational conversation with someone who has a schizophrenic personality?

#3: Start developing a sense of humor right now, because if you wait until they're 13, you will already be crazy. There is no way to make sense of their viewpoint.

#4: Every one deserves space of their own to manage as they please. Most parents have difficulty with this concept. If possible give your teen his/her own room so you don't have to look at it. If this is not financially viable, measure the room, divide it exactly in half, then place duct tape down the middle. I can from personal experience guarantee that within a week or two much energy will be expended to prove it was the other guy who was the slob all this time.

Verbalize the following conditions and put them into writing:

a. They must keep the door shut.

b. Anything that drifts out into common family space goes into the circular file.

c. Nothing can go in that mildews, rots, or attracts any kind of unwanted vermin, e.g., rats, mice, insects.

d. If he wants clothes washed, the clothes must come out of the room and be put into the clothes hamper. You do not want to stress yourself determining with a sniff test what is clean and what is dirty. The response to an hysterical, "Where are my favorite jeans?" is simply and calmly saying, "Gee, I don't remember seeing them in the clothes hamper."

#5: Homework. Provide a space and strict times. He must spend the time there without telephone or TV. Music may be okay. Negotiate as to type and volume. He can choose to use the time effectively or not. Failing to do homework may result in failing English. Both parent and teen need to understand that it is his decision alone. Based on his choices he may only need to learn a few phrases for his life's work. Maybe just six words, such as, "Would you like fries with that?" Or perhaps even just three, as in "Paper or plastic?"
Failing math may prevent him from ever being allowed near a cash register and thus never being promoted to manager at McDonalds. Remember, it is his ambition, not yours.

#6: Mealtimes. They can not complain about the food. They can't insult what you serve or call it dirty names, e.g., "chicken shit." They don't have to eat it. Be very suspicious if the family dog starts gaining weight. But there are no between-meal snacks unless they have eaten the main meal. Simply say, "You can take your allowance and go to the nearest restaurant of your choice." This saves you from a lot of upset meals. You don't have to hear, "I don't like that!" or "I don't want to eat veggies!"

#7: At monthly *mandatory* family meetings mutually agree on five rules and five consequences. These rules should be flexible during the time the teens' level of understanding is hopefully maturing and are governed by the following: Does it have a consequence on the whole family that is legal, financial, or emotional? Anything that has a consequence on the offender alone is allowed. That's how they learn and how they develop self esteem and critical thinking. Put the agreed rules on a large poster board. This will save you from screaming matches and also spare you from bursting the veins in your neck. You simply point to the offended rule, and ask quietly and unemotionally, "Did you do this? What is the consequence?" This is a great lesson in cause and effect.

This is also the meeting when household chores are determined. By mutual agreement place them on a calendar with large squares to accommodate the names. This is the opportunity to point without rancor, "Whose turn was it to empty the dish washer, or trash, etc.?" If you are fortunate you may find that some chores are favored and can become the permanent responsibility of one individual. It is unrealistic to expect that scrubbing toilets will ever be anyones favorite. Therefore it must fall into the "taking turns" section.

Consider that a long pointer in the form of a stick or a laser is a necessary household furnishing.

#8: The concept of allowance was meant to be a symbol that the child has value as a unique individual, and the money should not be subject to conditions but is a gift. Take away privileges, put your teen on restrictions if you must, but don't touch the allowance. We as human beings have difficulty experiencing unconditional love. An allowance is an attempt at an unconditional expression of that love.

A monthly clothing allowance, separate from a general allowance, can be spent at once or saved up. It can be a good lesson in money management. It will also spare you, if you're lucky, from hearing, "But everyone else is wearing ....!"

#9*:* Possible trade options. If all else fails, if you have friends or neighbors who are also going nuts with their teens, make a deal to swap children until they are old enough to be on their own. You will probably have become so much smarter and tolerable in their eyes that life together could be good again.

Remember you can't expect logical reasoning.

And good luck. May you live long and prosper. And may I not have to visit you at any mental health facility

HAIKU

trying to conform

I struggle five-seven-five

squelch creative juice

through my window scene

young buds forced form too early

will they ever bloom

can summer find me

spring so fickled moves in 'n' out

my skin longs for warmth

tall steel skeletons

precarious tilting cranes

clanging symphony

life blossoms bright now

long years of drought pass away

spring brings love anew

moonlight silhouetting

sleeping lovers

nights passions spent

(Southern California Haiku Study Group Anthology, 2012)

Bozana Belokosa

Bozana Belokosa has been published in fifteen local, national, and international poetry anthologies. She is the author of eight books. Her first book "What Happened to Rudolph's Nose?" is permanently housed in the "Burton Historical Collection for Michigan Authors" to be used by the public for reference. She is the founder of the "Organization of Black Screenwriters" founded in 1988. She is the creator, producer, director, host, and a performing poet on her own public access television show, "Spending A Little time With Poetry," which has been on the air for nine years.

THE POET

I am
A true poet
Writing a rhyme is fun
Which defines the greatest poet
I am

FAVORITE FOODS

Spinach is "Popeye" the sailor's symbolic semblance of strength

Which can be used to honor President Obama.

Its richness is complimentary to the wisdom of my grandmama.

Spinach possesses Obama's smiles' warmth and the power of
Uncle Saul,
Whenever, you eat it you are apt to grow big, strong, and tall.

It does not matter if you eat it alone or with someone else, to the
Excess.
Your huge desire for good ole spinach is never less.

Now when good ole spinach is served with liver and onions they
Cleave together,
And their combined goodness makes you want to massage your
Tummy until times get better.

Brown is the liver and the best onions are pure white.
The joys and delightful fulfillments these two foods give are
Dynamite.

"La-we-oh-me!"
"La-we-oh-me!"

When I eat fried liver and onions and compared it to my life I take
In a deep breath and exhale
Because one is so good and the other is like a fairy-tale.

Now after I ate the spinach, liver and onions I was served lime
Sherbet ice cream for the very first time.
I told my grandmama, "this is my favorite flavor, good ole lime!"

If I could put lime sherbet ice cream on a hidden shelf that would
Be divine,
But then I think you might say that wee child is quite asinine.

Before it is too late it's important for everyone to consume lime
Sherbet ice cream
Because it will lift your self-esteem like living the
American Dream,
And make you want to sing God Bless America!

DEATH'S MOURNING SONG

It came silently separating us.
Nothing can undo death.

Red tear eyes are lacing my lonely face
Because I am mourning death.

Overcoming grief may take all of my life
Missing you due to your death.

Bittersweet memories haunts all of me
Splashing letters spelling death.

Your ghost dances to our sweet sweet love song
Like you were dodging your death.

Sunrise and sunset will not be the same
After you left me for ole death.

SAINT ELIZABETH'S HOLY LITTLE CHAPEL

Located in Pasadena, CA

There is a little Catholic chapel where I go to pray

Within its walls I am totally at peace.

I get a good feeling that comforts me.

Everything is so clean.
None of the statues have dust on them.
A candle is always flickering in a red glass vase.
Somehow, I get the feeling everything is going to be okay
Because all is well.
I know whenever I come here God is present.
I know God is always glad to see me here.
There are always bouquets of fresh flowers perfuming the air.
This place is my home away from home.
Here the silence makes the most beautiful glorious music.
I feel the presence of the saints here.
I pray to my Saint Elizabeth and ask her for help and guidance.
Sometimes this place brings me to tears.
I weep not because I am sad, but because I have found happiness.
I weep for my soul and the souls of others.
I often think how being in a little Catholic chapel a person
Can be splashed with such pleasant vibrations.
I often think how a little sanctuary can make such beautiful
Kind loving thoughts dwell in my head
Then I realize this is the way it should be when you are in the
House of the Lord.
On my knees I always pray for others, for those who I feel have
Did me wrong or betrayed me.
In this holy chapel I ask God to bless everyone with longevity,
Good health and prosperity.
I ask for my forgiveness from God for all those I have wronged.

I ask God that I might be a bright light in the tunnel of life,
And when a train of people pass through my being might
Enlighten them by making their journey bright.
In this holy chapel I am at peace.
In this Godly place I try to leave the evil worldly thoughts I
May harbor within me outside of its doors.
In this chapel I am at one with the Lord.
My soul is embraced by the Holy Spirit.
This chapel makes me able to forgive my enemies whoever
They are.
No one can take away the good feelings I experience within the
Walls of this tiny chapel because they are now indelible
Precious memories.
Sometimes I long to be here in this chapel on the days I can not
Come because I have found solace and unity with God in
This little holy chapel which is my home away from home.

FAHRENHEIT 451

Technology is
Technology is
Technology is
Things we produce and things we use to get things done

Technology has been around
Technology has been around
Technology has been around
    Since the beginning of time
Technology can be
Technology can be
Technology can be
    Books, letters, computer software, a student's essay and
    Wall-Length televisions like those in *Fahrenheit 451*
Easily influenced
Easily influenced
Easily influenced
    By the unsound
Do not burn me
Do not burn me
Do not burn me
    I am technology making you more relevant; I am a book
What's a futuristic society
What's a futuristic society
What's a futuristic society
    Family television watchers; the anti-intellectual
A book is a loaded gun
A book is a loaded gun
A book is a loaded gun
        I am technology making you more relevant; I am a book

Easily influenced
Easily influenced
Easily influenced
By the unsound
Mindless
No kindness
Sadness
In a stupor
Sedated
Sleep it off
Sadness
Do not burn me
Steal me
Open me up
Read
Are your peepers open now?

TALES

Tales told about the soul
Impressed in gold on a scroll

Profound petals descending
Capturing experiences and defending.

Bits and pieces of this and that
Gained wisdom overflowing a hat,

Dropping on the ground
Scattering bygones all around.

Oh, to relive hours gone by
Or watch the yesterday's sun born on high

Perhaps dream a daydream again
And truly know your foe or friend in men.

Tales told about the soul
Revealing reveries to extol

Oh, be not spiritual dumbfound
As life compounds on its fatal merry-go-round.

THE ASHTRAY

I have contributed to some deaths.
I was not starving like some,
I helped die.
The fools replenished me constantly.
My belly was full and dirty;
But I felt no pain,
They did.
I destroyed.
I made them think they needed me.
Some took pride in seeing me dirty.
They emptied my butts, washed, and dried me.
Maybe they thought I would not kill them clean.
Ha, ha
The fools, coughed, could not breath, were cut on
And were sew on,
Also eventually died not even thinking of me.
I deserved some credit.
I helped too!
I was their ASHTRA

Cleopatra Natt

Cleopatra Natt graduated from Loyola Marymount University in Los Angeles, California with a degree in sociology.

Her plans are to attend graduate school for business and international relations. She would like to be an entrepreneur. She hopes to involve herself with efforts to save children from abuse and other negative experiences they may encounter.

Cleopatra tutored children in a wide range of subjects while in college and enjoyed it. She is also interested in further studying sociology; specifically culture, economics and education.

STORY TELLING

There was a little girl who was so tricky. She tricked her friends and made them feel unhappy sometimes. One day, she told her friends that she would like to meet them all in a group to tell them that she would be leaving town. She would be making a special trip to her grandparents who lived out of town. They all agreed on a time and place to meet. Despite the many tricks she had played, the girl really had to leave this time. It was not a trick. Her friends did not want her to leave. They wanted her to stay around so they could all play and run around. They expressed how much they were going to miss her.

The friends got together and discussed how they would really like to play a trick on this girl since she played tricks on them sometimes. They did not want to meet with her as a group because they were not sure if she would really show up. However, they couldn't be as tricky as their friend. They liked their friend enough to meet just one more time, whether it was a trick or a treat. The girls got little snacks and made lemonade for the meeting. The tricky girl also went out to buy some snacks for the meeting because she wanted to show her friends how much she would miss them. She felt very sorry for how she had tricked her friends before and wasn't sure if she would make new friends while she was with her grandparents.

The day finally came for this girl to meet with her friends. "Is she coming or not?" her friends all thought. They took all their snacks and lemonade to the meeting and set up. The girl came running to the meeting with her snacks. She told her friends that she was going to live with her grandparents because they needed help. She wouldn't be returning to her parents soon. They laughed, ate and played games. It was really fun.

They all went home happy. She told her friends how much she was going to miss them and they told her how much they were going to miss her. They gave her a very pretty address book with their names, addresses and telephone numbers.

The lesson to learn from this story is to be true to yourself and your friends.

EXCERPTS FROM: HOW I LEARNED TO READ
I Read The Street Signs On The Way To School

As a Preschooler and a Kindergartener, I learned how to read by starting with the street signs. The ride to school was long. My parents drove me to school using the streets instead of the highway or freeway. I didn't want to just sit in the car without being busy. My parents were busy driving me and I chose to stay busy reading.

I learned how to count, so the street numbers were not difficult to say. The names of the streets were difficult at times for me, though. I tried to pronounce the names of the streets as best I could. If I couldn't pronounce the words, I asked my parents to help. As much as my parents were always happy to help me read, I wanted to figure out words on my own. I looked forward to the fun activity of reading every day.

When I got to the name of a street that was long, I took out a piece of paper and pencil to write down the name. I spelled the name of the street and showed it to my parents and they pronounced it for me. I said the name over and over until I learned how to say it right. I also read names of stores, the stop signs, the train tracks, and construction signs like "detour". I learned that the red light means "stop" and the green light means "go". I also learned that the yellow light means one should be cautious, careful or slow down and get ready to stop. The flashing red light also means stop and then you may keep going when it is safe to do so.

I learned to always look on your left-hand side and on your right-hand side to see if it is safe to go. The flashing yellow lights also mean be careful and get ready to stop. I saw a red hand and a white hand that were the street signs for a crosswalk. The red hand means that I cannot cross the street and the white hand means that I can cross the street. The crosswalk is a safe place to walk when crossing the street. The crosswalk looks like a hopscotch sign. I learned how to play hopscotch in school and it reminded me of the crosswalk. I saw another sign that was yellow with a picture of two people on it. I learned that the sign means that you are near a school and you must stop when children are crossing. Sometimes there is a "Safety Patrol" person at the crosswalk to help children cross the street. The "Safety Patrol" person stops all the cars to help the children cross the street. Sometimes parents or guardians walk their children to school and they help them cross the street in the crosswalk.

On my way to school, I also read signs that were on the stores, houses, on the buses, cars, billboards and just anything that was close enough to read on my way to school. Some cars advertise businesses like the telephone companies, gas companies, water and power companies, plumbing companies and the linen washing companies. Some cars advertise themselves with "for sale" signs.

I read signs on the big public bus that advertised movies and T.V. shows. I read real estate signs that were selling houses. I read signs that said "apartment for rent". There were many school buildings on the way to my school and I read their names. Some of the schools were elementary, middle and high. I even passed by colleges and universities on my way to school.

***

I ASKED MY PARENTS TO BUY ME BOOKS INSTEAD OF CANDY OR TOYS.

Parents usually take their kids with them to the store, the bank, the laundromat and many other places because they don't have babysitters. Babysitters are people you trust to leave your kids with. They are usually paid to take care of kids and they can be expensive. My parents left me at the day care center where the babysitter lived.

They took me with them to the store to buy groceries. Some kids pick up things and cry in order to make their parents buy them these things. Sometimes the parents don't have enough money to buy the extra things that their kids pick up and put in the shopping cart. Some parents have a budget and they make a list of the things they plan to buy.

When kids pick up candy, cookies and toys that are not on the list, and the parents don't buy them, then the kids cry. The kids think that crying will make the parents buy what they want. It might work with some parents, but it doesn't work with most.

What I always asked for when I went to the store with my parents was not candy, cookies or toys. I asked my parents to buy me books, because I liked to read. My parents were very surprised that I asked for books and they were very glad to buy me them. They did not expect me to pick up books. They were glad that I asked for books and were glad to buy them.

GIVING BACK

Remember, when someone
Took you to school and picked you up?
Remember, the teacher who taught you
How to read and write when you
Didn't understand the schoolwork?

A parent or guardian drove you
To the doctor when you got so sick
And could not really help yourself?

A friend might have shared
His lunch with you when you forgot
Your lunch or simply didn't have any
How about that favor you needed
When times were tough?
Oh! I'll pay you back, but never did

Too many people have helped you
On your almost-impossible journey
To success and excellence

So, what do you do now
When you have met your goals
And all your accomplishments too?
Give back to those who are now
In need like you once were
Give back and make the world
A better place for all
Give back like there was no tomorrow
Give, give, give back until it hurts

Connie Bessman-Natt

Connie Bessman-Natt is a high school teacher and college guidance counselor with the Los Angeles Unified School District. She is committed to making a difference in the lives of children all over the world. She is an advocate for inner-city students. Her goal is to assist children to achieve academically.

NEVER GIVE UP ON YOUR DREAMS

Never give up on your dreams, no matter what. You should continue to work on these dreams all the time. You are driven by that particular dream until you reach the goal. You live, sleep, eat, play and always think about that dream. That dream is like a thing that just nags at you always. You are not satisfied or really happy until that dream is fulfilled. Preparation will definitely help that dream. It doesn't just magically happen. Preparation and opportunity will successfully make the dream a reality.

There once was a child who dreamed about becoming a doctor. She was passionate about one day healing people all over the world. She didn't know how this goal would be accomplished. All she had was the will. She believed that where there is a will, there is a way. This kid made good grades in school and enrolled in programs that were associated with healthcare and joined health related clubs in school. She was involved in internship programs which were both paid and unpaid. She volunteered in hospitals, clinics and research programs. This child liked science and was very interested in any thing that involved science.

This child excelled in science and received many awards from science fairs and projects. She participated in many science camps and programs, learning from the experiences of the doctors, nurses and other healthcare professionals. The kid was very curious and always asked questions. Asking questions is a good way to learn, and this kid did just that. This child is well on the path to fulfilling the dream.

Another child dreamed about becoming a musician and started learning how to play the piano at age four. He enrolled in piano classes. He also learned how to play by asking his mom to teach him how to play the piano. His mother had a little experience in playing the piano and she used that to help her son. Mom taught him, but that was not enough for the kid, so he continuously learned from YouTube. This kid got further help by teaching himself. He also has excellent architectural skills, demonstrated by building Lego structures. He makes good grades in school.

Yet another child dreams about becoming a professional basketball player. At age five, he played ball outside with his friends, his dad, and anyone who wanted to play basketball with him. He even played ball in the house when nobody was looking and broke quite a number of windows, picture frames, furniture and dishes. This kid loves school and makes good grades because failure is not an option to him. A supportive family is also a contributing factor to this child's success.

In preparation for reaching his goal and to successfully make his dream come true, the kid played in tournaments, practiced with professional trainers and played on school teams. This kid is a real "gym rat". His drive, determination, perseverance and hard work in school will help him succeed.

* * *

MAKING A DIFFERENCE

When was the last time you tried to make a difference in the life of anyone?

The ability to make a difference has no age requirement, boundary or size. A child can make a difference on the playground by playing fair, in class by exhibiting good behavior to teachers, classmates, and everywhere else by respecting others. Sharing also plays a big part in making a difference.

Share with the unfortunate, the struggling, the elderly and the sick. It does not necessarily take the whole world to make a difference because one person can make a difference in the lives of many.

A teacher made a difference in the lives of so many children. She was not wealthy enough to give them silver or gold, but she gave them the "wealth" of love, kindness, and compassion. She offered smiles, focus, determination, study habits, tutorial assistance, life skills and more. Kids left her classroom with a wealth of knowledge, wisdom and common sense. She listened to the children and their families. She did not avoid the kids or turn them away. The kids and their families always came back to say "hi", even after they graduated.

This teacher voluntarily tutored kids who were struggling academically by providing more resources and opportunities to be able to succeed. She made referrals to summer programs, job internships and college preparation programs. This teacher did all that she could do to make positive things happen for the children. She demonstrated great attendance, because she wanted to teach the life lesson of being present to learn. She wanted to lead by example and show the kids that they had to be present, by being present herself. She visited her students when they were sick and missed school. She gave them incentives to do well and celebrated their big or small accomplishments. She followed through on her end with everything she could do to further their educational plans.

BREAKS

Summer breaks, Thanksgiving breaks, Christmas breaks,
Spring breaks and all the other breaks that fall in between
Are all good for children and their families to rest and regroup.

These breaks should be meaningful and life lessons learned
For the stress, and all the time that has been burned
Take short or long trips if you can
View other environments that are different from yours

Attend a camp of some sort that will get rid of the bores
From school, work, illness and just take a tour
It may be a sports camp, hiking camp or it may be
Just a camp to discover the beauty of nature
Those memories will always be yours forever.

Find programs that will teach you skills like art, sports and more.
Academic programs will definitely open many, many doors.
Breaks are also a good time to catch up on classes that you need,
To be able to graduate from that long journey of school.
It is also a good time to experience the joy of the working world.

ALL MY FRIENDS AND I

All my friends and I are in one big circle,
Just doing the things that we like to do.
We talk, laugh and share jokes too.

Friends are there for each other,
In good times and bad times.
They support, encourage and care.
They reach out to others,
And understand in such a way,
That is so amazing as if they,
Could read the minds of people.

We work and work so hard,
We send out greeting cards
To keep us and others encouraged
For we know what we have to unfold
Our families and the whole wide world.

We try not to look tired,
We're actually burned down to the wire.
To all my friends I would like to say,
Hang in there, whatever the cost may.

EARTH'S TREASURES

Earth's treasures cannot be measured
They may be found everywhere
In the rivers, the ocean and on the land.
Mines also carry these great treasures
Precious stones spit out bright gems
How can you really reach them?

Crystals, agates, quartz, diamonds,
Gold, amethyst, turquoise and opal are bold.
Earth's treasures have no measures
For they have been around forever.

All of the beauty from these bright creatures,
Have lifted up spirits with such great pleasure.
These treasures are used for
Rings, charms, watches, necklaces,
Belts, earrings, bags and bling-blings.

Earth's treasures cannot be measured
You can even find them in the desert.
They may look so very rough,
But some water and a little polish
Will put a shine and make them fine.

BE YOURSELF

Fake, phony, pretense or deception,
You better hope to get any reception.
You don't have to fit in.

Just be your true self,
'cause you will be loved just the same.
If you just be your own true self.

Be true blue. Be who you really are
Be unique. Be one of a kind.
Be yourself, be true, be real
For you could land a great big deal
By just being very, very real.

UNITED WE STAND

Whether it's at home, school or work,
You must unite to make things happen
Unity will bring dignity
To those who really care

It doesn't take much to make a change
What is needed is unity, togetherness and peace
Yes, united we stand, divided we fall

Don't you want to be united?
At home, work, school or wherever you are?
It only brings change to everyone

Complaining and loud talking, blowing and biting
Will really get you nowhere
If you do nothing about it

You have to stand in unity
For a positive change to happen
Because unity does bring dignity
Here, there and everywhere

DON'T MARRY BECAUSE....

Don't marry because she's cute or he's cute
Don't marry because everyone says
You look so good together
Everyone will not live in the home with you
And experience the problems that follow
Don't marry because one has too much money
Disappointment is about to hit you, honey
Don't marry to be taken care of
More disappointment is on the rise

Arrangements may work sometimes
But it depends on what's on your mind
Prepare yourself for better or worse
Not knowing what's in the purse
Love the one you marry
But please make sure you are also loved
It is not a one way street
Or you will experience a big defeat
Don't let the sweet talk fool you
Infatuation is a really sad thing
That should cause your mind to think
Don't marry because of sympathy
Even those may seriously disappoint you
You may get burned from actions
That you thought were being cautioned

Don't marry just because
Please put your reasons on pause
Until you realize what it will really cause
Just don't marry because………

BUSTED

Have you ever been busted, caught on the spot, just seen doing something that is not right or you really have no business doing? It is similar to a child's hand being caught in the cookie jar. "I wasn't taking a cookie. I was just trying to rearrange the cookies." That's what the response might sound like, even when the cookie was in the hand and on the way to the mouth.

What if you were caught cheating on a test? What would your reaction be if the teacher walked by and just took away your paper while your classmates were watching?

Develop study skills in school so that you will be able to study in advance for examinations. Take good notes and compare them with the teacher's notes or those of your study buddies. Form study groups. Use resources like the libraries or set aside a study spot at home. Sacrifice time to study.

This one is a very common example of really getting busted. Couples, who claim that they are committed, but are caught with others, do not usually know how to explain the embarrassment. They make excuses and try to cover up one lie on top of another. It doesn't add up, but you try all you can to make it.

What can you do to make all of that up? Apologize and not do it again? Talk about it? Get professional help? That is all good, but are you really sorry or you're upset because you got busted? Be responsible. Be committed if that's what you choose to be. Always communicate.

United we stand!

Dan Lambert

Dan Lambert is a writer and educator from Inglewood, California. He holds a master's degree in English from Loyola Marymount University. He also holds a bachelor's degree in History from Loyola Marymount University and an associate degree in History from El Camino College.

Dan has taught English at East Los Angeles College since 2000. He has taught Literature online for Colorado Technical University since 2010. He has also taught English at Pasadena City College, Santa Monica College, California State University at Dominguez Hills, Langston University, DeVry University, West Los Angeles College, Los Angeles Southwest College, Los Angeles City College, and Harbor College.

Dan's writing appears in such publications as *Easy Reader, Torrance People, Other Worlds, Wrapped in Plastic,* and *Games Unplugged.* His poetry appears in the anthologies *An Island of Egrets, Faces of Love, Tales on the Twisted Side,* and *Sci Fi Fan II.* He is a regular contributor to *The Sorcerer's Scrolls* (a role-playing gaming magazine) and *The Write Stuff!* (the newsletter of The Southwest Manuscripters). He is the winner of the Shakespeare Award for his poem, "My Ode to Joy."
Please visit Dan's Web site at
http://dan_lambert.homestead.com/

THE AFTERVERSE: A ROMP INTO THE ETHER

(Chapter One: The Discombobulation)

By Dan Lambert

The circumstances of my accident and subsequent death - the stuff that made the newspapers - will only be briefly addressed in the report you are about to read. Never mind that I am dead. I know what you're thinking: how can the dead tell stories about their lives from beyond the grave? Have you ever seen the movie *Sunset Boulevard?* It goes something like that. It just happens, and it just works. I could explain the technicalities of it to you, but I guarantee that the knowledge would be lost on you. You are, after all, alive. No offense, but you are ignorant by the very definition of your existence. You see, everyone gains a certain level of clarity - an insight into the workings of the Universe - when they die. You are not there yet, which pleases me. You should be in no hurry to meet the reaper, although you will soon see that my wife was most definitely in a hurry to meet him after learning that he had claimed me.

But forgive me. I'm getting ahead of myself. If you care to read more about the way I died - and the person who (accidentally) killed me - I suggest you take a look at the online archives of the *Razor Hat Gazette:* God knows all the gory details are there. What is not there is the way I felt about dying, not to mention the way I still feel about it. What is all this about feelings, you might ask. When people die, don't they just snuff out like a flame that has used up its fuel? Not to get all religious on you, but that is far from the truth. The truth is that the Afterlife exists: not so much as a Heaven and a Hell with angels and demons, respectively. The Afterlife is more like the hall of mirrors at your neighborhood fun house.

So, when I passed on to the next world, it wasn't so much like blinking out, but like waking up in a recovery room after major surgery. There I was, in a beautiful field of poppies, with a little white lamb licking my face. I rubbed my eyes like characters do in those old Warner Brothers cartoons, and had a look at my surroundings. There was nothing but rolling, green fields of soft grass and flowers in all directions. The lamb kept licking. A small, brass bell was tied around its neck with a scarlet length of silk. The bell tinkled softly as the lamb licked.

"Stop it," I said. "That tickles."

The lamb stopped licking. "I'm sorry," it said in a soft, feminine, breathy, Marilyn Monroe voice.

I paused. My last memory before waking up in the field was being flattened by a delivery truck in the middle of Milhaus Avenue, the main thoroughfare in my home town of Razor Hat, Illinois. Razor Hat is the only town in the United States named after a James Bond villain. At least, that was the intention when Mayor Wallace Kato officially changed the town's name from Nickel Card to Razor Hat. The actor who had played Odd Job in an old James Bond film stopped in town back in 1983. In case you don't remember (or just don't go to movies), Odd Job used a razor-edged hat to decapitate his enemies. Mayor Kato didn't realize that the character's name was Odd Job: he just always assumed the guy was named Razor Hat. Also, Mayor Kato never bothered to ask the actor what his name was. Anyway, Kato changed our town's name to Razor Hat, and the name caught on like wildfire. There's even a restaurant shaped like a big, black hat out on Milhaus Avenue, right down the street from where the truck hit me.

I must have been knocked cold. I was having one hell of a bizarre dream.

Okay, I'll play along, I decided. "Where am I?" I asked the lamb. "Who are you?"

The lamb smiled. It would have made sense in an animated Disney film. In three dimensions, it was just unsettling. "My name is Sydney. Welcome to the Plain of Newcomers, Newcomer! Your name is Robert Mist."

"Thank you," I said incredulously. "I know my own name. So, what is the Plain of Newcomers? Wait a minute. Did you say Sydney? With a 'y'? This is a funny dream. That's my wife's name."

The lamb sat on her white-and-pink haunches. "You're not dreaming, dear. And it's me: Sydney. With a 'y'."

I sat up. My face was the very epitome of incredulousness. "What do you mean? You're a damn talking lamb. You're not my wife."

"I am so your wife," the Syd-lamb said. "And what have I told you about taking the Lord's name in vain?"

Jesus Christ and His Shadow. A talking lamb telling me it was my wife. What kind of drugs did the emergency room doctors give me? Was I hit by a truck hauling LSD samples? What was going on? I decided to play along. Lucid dreaming could be amusing. I sometimes used it as a brainstorming technique in my classes at Razor Hat Community College. "Okay, lamb. I'll bite: you are my wife, Sydney Collins-Mist. So, Syd; it's nice to see you here. What's with the Marilyn Monroe voice?"

I had never seen an animal blush, but the lamb that was badly impersonating my wife did just that. "Oh, that! Do you like it? We can choose any voice we like, you know." She glanced down at her wooly body. "And anybody we like. I chose a lamb with a Marilyn Monroe voice. Why did you choose to look and sound like a grizzly bear?"

What the hell? I stood up, and brushed the green grass stains from my body. I was a good eight feet tall, and covered in brown fur. I was either a bear or wearing a really good bear suit. This dream was getting weirder by the second. The unnerving part was that it was getting more realistic too. It lacked all the signature fuzziness of my previous dreams.

"Okay. I'm a bear and you're a lamb, right? And you say you are Sydney, my wife."

The lamb nodded. "I am your wife, dear. I'm a lamb and you're a bear. More precisely, I chose the form of a lamb and the voice of Marilyn Monroe, because (as you know) *Bus Stop* is my favorite movie, and – I don't know! – Little lambs are so cute! The question is, why did you choose a bear? You probably chose a bear because Teddy Roosevelt is your favorite president, and you prized that cast-iron bank with Teddy shooting a grizzly bear. And the growly voice... I don't know. Did you choose it because it sounds sexy? Because it does, you know. By the way, Robert, you didn't answer my question. Why the bear?"

'I have no idea," I said. "I'm a bear and you're a lamb. This must be some kind of weird fever dream, because there is lots of stuff about the universe I don't know. But I'm damn sure that bears don't talk. And I'm equally sure that little sheep, as cute and white and fluffy as you are, do not talk."

She seemed flattered. She said so.

"You're welcome," I responded.

I was starting to figure out the situation. Or so I thought. I decided to accept the idea that this fluffy animal before me was Sydney Collins, now Sydney Collins-Mist, my wife of three years. I mean, she had the body of a lamb, but the eyes did vaguely remind me of Sydney. The whole dream had an absurdist, Disneyesque quality to it, but the dream's environment was more like a Technicolor, three-dimensional virtual reality ride: the endless, rolling hills of grass met an orange, cloudy horizon. Sydney's wooly body (as well as my brown, furry one) stood out in stark contrast to the green grass, and the fresh smell in the air – the ozone smell that hangs in the air after a thunderstorm – was as strong and vivid as the smell of perfume in a whorehouse. Sydney was telling me this was real, and it certainly seemed real (if not altogether familiar or authentic) to me. I continued the conversation. "So, we get to choose the way we look and sound in our dreams, or whatever this is?"

Sydney grinned with her little, red lamb mouth, and then spoke in that sultry voice. This time, she sounded grave. "Oh no, Dear. This is not a dream. This is the Afterlife. We are on the Plain of Newcomers. I know it. I did my research before I crossed over."

This brought up more questions than it answered, but I was getting used to it. "The Afterlife? So Syd, honey bunny: are you saying that we're both dead?"

"Oh, yes, Robert." Again with the graveness. "Don't you remember the truck?"

"Well, yeah. Are you saying that the truck ran me over and killed me?" I was getting a terrible itch in the middle of my furry back. I tried to reach back and scratch it, when I noticed that my hands were, in fact, furry paws ending in curved claws. What was it bears did in the wild? I saw a mechanical bear do it once at Disneyland: they scratched their backs on tree trunks. But there were no tree trunks as far as the eye could see.

I focused on Sydney. "Okay, so I'm dead. I was hit by a truck. But that doesn't explain why you are here. You were at your aerobics class when I was hit. I was tipsy and coming out of Mulligan's Pub at 9 pm, and I know for a fact that your aerobics class doesn't let out until 10 pm. Besides, if this is

Heaven, why does my back itch? Why aren't there any trees that I can scratch it on?"

Sydney rose on all fours and arched her back. She then craned her lamb neck to look up at me. I felt bad for her, so I got down on my forepaws. We were eye to eye. "Robert, Honey: I couldn't bear to look at your rifle after that truck driver killed you. I carried it out to the garage, but I tripped. I accidentally shot myself in the head with that .22 rifle that you used to kill those poor, defenseless rabbits. Honestly, Honey: how many times have I told you to unload that thing before you put it away? Anyway, do you remember how I carried on when I found you skinning that rabbit in the kitchen? I thought this kind of thing would result in lots more blood, and you know how hard blood stains are to get out of our towels, let alone our carpeting!"

I couldn't believe what I was hearing. Suddenly, the fact that my wife and I had transformed into rejects from a *Bambi* movie was secondary in my mind. I was killed by a truck, and Syd had shot herself while carrying my rifle. I was getting dizzy. I had to slow down. I had to slow her down. "Wait, wait, wait!" I said. I felt a bit less dizzy. "Okay, Syd... Go on."

She continued: "After you died, I did research on the Afterlife. I was worried that when I died, I might get hung up on a seemingly-trivial technicality. For instance, what if you ended up in Heaven and I ended up in Hell? I wouldn't be at all useful to you if that had happened."

Useful?

"Anyway, I checked out that copy of the *Necronomicon* from the library. You know the one: the one you are always using in your Horror 101 class." For those of you who don't know, the *Necronomicon* is similar to the Tibetan Book of the Dead. It is supposed to contain secrets about life and death, and it also foretells the return of deadly creatures known as the Old Ones. The Old Ones are supposed to drive humans off the Earth someday, and reclaim the planet as their own. Dark and disturbing stuff. The problem is this: the *Necronomicon* doesn't exist. It was invented by a fiction writer.

I interrupted her. "Syd, Honey: don't you know what I always tell you? The *Necronomicon* was invented by H.P. Lovecraft, a writer of fiction. That book is no more real than the Emerald City or *Mary Poppins.* That English translation in the Razor Hat Public Library is one of many so-called *Necronomicons* written by various self-appointed new age gurus."

Syd had been Head Research Librarian at the Razor Hat Public Library for more than fifteen years. She nodded her little lamb head. "I know all that, Robert. But Honey: the Neconomicon in our library was written by no ordinary guru. It was written by Nathan Twist. I did lots of research on Twist. He visited Lovecraft in Providence in 1923, and found out that the *Necronomicon* was real. It had been passed down through generations by the original author's descendants."

I nodded my big bear head as Syd spoke. As a professor of English at Razor Hat Community College, I had specialized in the horror literature and macabre fiction. Lovecraft was one of my favorite authors. According to him, the *Necronomicon* was written centuries ago by Abdul Alhazred, also known as "The Mad Arab." It was translated into English by Dr. John Dee in the seventeenth century. It was supposed to contain all the dark secrets of this life and the next: enough secrets to threaten the sanity of anyone who dared to read it cover-to-cover. But that was all fiction concocted by Lovecraft for the pulps in the 1920s and 1930s. Or was it?

Syd paused to emit a sheep-like "baa" sound, and then continued. Did we get to make animal sounds as well as use human speech? Did this mean I could growl? "Anyway," she said, "to make a long story short, after talking with Lovecraft, Twist discovered that every word of the *Necronomicon* was true. Lovecraft loaned Twist a copy of Dee's manuscript, which Twist translated into modern English. Fifty years later, in 1973, Pinewood Press published the *Necronomicon* as part of their *Mysteries of Life and Death* series."

I knew that Josephus Pinewood dropped out of Berkeley in 1969, and started Pinewood Press the following year. Pinewood was one of the leading publishers of so-called "New Age" books: stuff about every unexplained occurrence from Bigfoot to the Loch Ness Monster. The *Necronomicon* we kept in the Razor Hat Public Library was one of the Pinewood Press editions, edited and with an introduction by Josephus Pinewood. I had used it many times in my Horror 101 class at Razor Hat Community College. Aside from an occasional Goth kid every Halloween, nobody else checked it out except for me. And now, it turns out that my dead wife – who had chosen to take the form of a lamb and the voice of Marilyn Monroe in the Afterlife – had checked it out and used it to research life after death before accidentally blowing her brains out with my hunting rifle. It was enough to make me want that truck to take another swipe at me.

"But Honey," I asked. "Sweetie Pie: what did you learn about the Afterlife from the *Necronomicon*? And can any of that knowledge help us to figure out where we are and what is going on?"

I should have known Sydney would have a good answer. Why do you think I married her? "A pretty face and brains too," I used to tell her. I fell in love the moment I laid eyes on her, which was way back when we were both freshman at Razor Hat High School (Go Sharpies!) There was just something about the way Sydney moved back then. I would always tell her she was like Jello on springs, to quote Jack Lemmon's commentary on Marilyn Monroe's saunter in the film *Some Like It Hot.* It wasn't until after our senior year, right before graduation, that Syd told me that Marilyn Monroe was her favorite actress. There were so many happy coincidences in our lives together. We were even born on the same day: October 22, 1969. And now we were both animals out of some fever dream, roaming a bright green, treeless plain in the Afterlife.

Sydney cleared her throat and looked at me in a way that was not at all sheep-like, but definitely reminded me of the way the human Sydney Collins-Mist had looked at me. This was Sydney, all right. "First of all," she said, "forget everything we learned in Catholic school about Heaven and hell. We all end up right here, Robert: on the Field of Newcomers. Hell and Heaven can be reached from here, if we choose to visit those places. But Robert, Heaven and hell are just signposts on a much larger landscape. The Afterlife is huge, and – like Walt Whitman – it contains multitudes. We can go wherever we like! We can subconsciously choose our physical forms, and our voices, from the myriad of images and voices stored in our unconscious minds at the moments of our deaths. Do you remember the mistake Dan Ackroyd made in *Ghostbusters*?"

I nodded my big bear head. Of course I remembered. Syd knew this was one movie we both loved with a passion. Ackroyd and the other Ghostbusters are asked to choose the form of the monster that destroys New York – and then the world. Everyone tries to clear their minds, but Ackroyd's character accidentally thinks about the Stay-Puft Marshmallow Man – a friendly character from his childhood. Consequently, the evil god appears as this huge, white, fluffy marshmallow man with a hideously jolly grin, and proceeds to destroy the city. I saw where Syd was going with this: Ackroyd chose the form of his tormentor, and we – at the moment of death– chose the forms of our Afterlife bodies. It all made sense, but it didn't jive with the Heaven-and-hell Afterlife that we learned about in Sunday school.

I scratched my bear head with my bear claw. "Syd, Honey: I believe everything you're saying. But why couldn't you go on without me? And why were you already here when I woke up? Where do we go from here? What do we do?"

Sydney sighed. My wife had indeed taken the form of a lamb, but she was still beautiful to my new bear eyes. And I still loved her more than ever. "My Love," she said, "time takes on a whole new meaning here on the other side of death. Notice that there is no sun in the sky." There wasn't. There was nothing but a vague orange light behind the clouds. Sydney sat back on her haunches once again. "Robert, it is true that you died before I did. You died a full three days before I did. You were in a coma for more than twenty-four hours, in fact. I prayed that you would come out of it. Oh, how I prayed. But when I was sure you would not come out of it, I read the *Necronomicon*. I read it very carefully. The first thing I learned is that a soul who dies without intending it – someone like you – comes to the Plain of Newcomers asleep. They then gradually wake up in a green field, like you did. Someone who dies intentionally comes to the Plain fully awake. Somebody Up There must have mistaken me for a suicide. I found you sleeping, and knew you would soon awaken, but souls wake up faster when a loved one greets them, as I did when I licked your face. Honey, I came here three days after you arrived, but you were asleep here for every second of those three days."

I grunted and groaned. Syd smiled as if she could read my thoughts. "Honey, I didn't mean to shoot myself, but now that I'm here with you, I'm happy. I think the reason I left our world to join you here is very important. In fact, it is the single most important thing I learned from Nathan Twist's translation of the *Necronomicon*. Robert, I came here to help you. There are problems here in the Afterlife, Robert. Take the Plain of Newcomers, for example. It is scheduled to be destroyed in three Earth days, which go by much faster on this side of the Veil."

I didn't know what to make of any of this. "The Veil?" I asked. I think I already knew the answer.

"The Veil between life and death," Sydney said. "Robert, you are the only person – the only soul – capable of saving the Plain of Newcomers. If the Plain is destroyed, the dead will begin to seep back into the living world, and the living will come here. You must save the Plain, but you cannot do it alone. That's why I killed myself, Robert: so I could come here and help you."

We set out in the direction of the largest cloud. This direction was called leeward, at least according to what Sydney had remembered from her reading of the *Necronomicon*. As Syd and I walked and talked, her small lamb frame somehow keeping up with the long reach of my bear legs, I realized that I was way in over my head with this Afterlife business. Syd was the one with the knowledge. But, then again: what was I risking, my life?

(To be continued.....)

Faith Beckerman Goldman

Faith Beckerman Goldman is a natural storyteller and enjoys weaving the threads from many parts of her life experience. From her roots in Connecticut with a large, colorful family to serving as a physical therapist for more than 30 years to surviving breast cancer with gusto to creating a family memoir and historical narrative about her late husband's life as a Jewish boy raised in the ghettos of Shanghai (*Slow Boat From and to China*) – Faith captures everyday moments and makes them personal and memorable.

Faith relishes the many roles that have shaped her unique point of view. Wife, mother to two grown children, physical therapist and rehabilitation director, speaker on Jewish history, successful baking entrepreneur at *Faith's Sweet Creations*, community volunteer, Temple Menorah Sisterhood Board member and winner of her congregation's 2009 Woman of the Year Award. Faith is a published expert in the physical therapy arena and is a regular contributor chronicling community life for *The Daily Breeze*. She has also has been profiled in local, national and international media in the U.S., Israel and China on her historical work on the Shanghai Jews.

"I've always taken notice of the details – the smells in my mom's kitchen, the tattoo art of a patient, the positioning of cracks in the sidewalk – and tried to paint a picture that draws the reader into my world. For me, I love that writing can enlighten, educate, entertain and provide a powerful sense of catharsis."

THE APPRECIATION OF A SWEET POTATO

It was 1945 in a small Connecticut town called Danbury. I was born prematurely and, at age 2 & ½, I was still underweight. With a precious food ration, my Mother bought a large sweet potato. It was presented to me hot from the oven with crackling skin, the orange flesh donned with oleo, and a sweet whiff of cinnamon was in the air. But my body language said no. Mom said "Do you know that there are Jewish children starving in China?" Little did we know then that one of those children was my husband to be. He, along with 18,000 Jewish refugees, was interned in a ghetto in Shanghai for two and-a-half years. Those that survived were liberated by the American Armed forces in late August of 1945.

Robert Goldman, age five, stood in a soup kitchen line with his Mother Thea to get one sweet potato. Record keeping was very efficient – your name was crossed off when you received your daily starch. Robert ate his very fast. Why? Because he was afraid someone was going to steal it. Still hungry, he quietly went into another line and took someone else's hand. He confidently approached the one in charge, gave his name, was told no, and then slapped. Until his untimely passing in 1994, Robert never ate a sweet potato after the war. Why? Because he didn't have to.

At the same war time, my now boyfriend Harry Fischman, was taken from Romania by cattle car May 1944 to Auschwitz. Of all of his family, Harry and his brother Manny were the only ones to survive at time of Liberation April 11, 1945. The brothers, age 14 and 16, worked in a labor camp. One of Harry's jobs was to help carry a large kettle of soup to the workers. The soup was clear with some mysterious grain in it later to be identified as bone meal. While all were busy eating, Harry roamed around to the back of the kitchen. There in front of him were piles of raw potatoes behind a fence. With a skinny stick, Harry attempted to urge one potato to roll under the fence. He was stopped in his tracks by a work supervisor called a *Kapo.* The punishment for stealing was to be a public hanging in the morning. With some stroke of luck, another official who recognized Harry said "Let him go. He actually didn't get the potato."

My love then was a 70-pound youth at time of liberation. Now Harry eats a sweet potato with great relish and time. Manned with several utensils, he slowly consumes every bit of the flesh. I get the skin so as not to waste a bit. At certain times he is quiet at dinner, his eyes telling me he is reflecting back to the past. I wait.

***

THE MOURNING/MORNING OF BROKEN GLASS

It was 6:00 a.m. in the morning of Sept. 11, 2001 and my aches and pains were interrupting my sleep. Sometimes I'll stretch or read my mail. And then doze again. I never watch TV in the daytime so I was unaware of the day's devastation.

The 1st piece of mail was a padded envelope from a Jewish organization that sends a memorial candle for the New Year. But this package was crumbled and the insides shook. Upon opening, I saw that the outside glass container was in a million pieces. I was sad about that when the phone rang, startling me. My friend said "Turn on the news. America is being attacked!" And we were. Then my son Sam called who was working out at a local gym beefing up as he had just enlisted in the U.S. Army 3 weeks earlier. And my daughter Naomi called saying she'd be at my home in 30 minutes as she lives 1/2 a block from the Federal Building in West L.A. We need to be together! Within seconds, the broken glass in my hands was not just an accident but a symbol yet to be defined.

I wasn't born yet but I had heard firsthand accounts about November 9/10, 1938 – *Kristallnacht* – the night of broken glass. My beau of then 6 years is a child survivor of the Holocaust. My knowledge of the war expanded as I shared with Harry my late husband's wartime in Shanghai. Synagogues, Jewish businesses, books were all being burned by the Nazis in Germany. The full WW11 hadn't started yet. The feelings were the same – broken glass, broken dreams, broken lives, anxiety, fear of the unknown – but what was not and has not been broken are our spirit and our faith to go on. The simultaneous activity of my broken glass and the shattering of lives that had flashed across the screen were not to be believed by me.

I spoke at a healing service on September 12, 2001 at Temple Menorah in Redondo Beach, California. So did my son who was now more committed in his decision to join the Army. Unlike his late father Robert who was drafted in order to become a U.S. citizen, Sam enlisted and his words were clear. "I have joined the Army to support and defend the Constitution of the United States, to live up to my potential, and to make everyone, including myself, proud." Sam's sister Naomi and hundreds of attendees that evening felt a little safer knowing one in our community was going to be serving.

We gathered to help put the pieces of broken glass together. We knew this job could not be hurried. We also cannot forget that the lines between the broken pieces would always be visible. Our prayers were silent, tearful, together, and have not been for naught.

Yes, it's ten years later and the 3,000 names may have faded to those not directly related. Just as the number 6 million Jews lost in the Holocaust is overwhelming, it's not 6 million – it's one and one and one. Not 3,000 but one and one and one.

My son served for 8 years and saw a tour of duty in South Korea. He did make a difference through his position and duties.

On August 23rd, 2011, we flew into New York City. There jutting into the night sky was the almost completed 9/11 Memorial. Stronger, bigger, more visible than ever. We are stronger; our agencies are working together, we are more aware, and must never forget! 9/11 is a day on a calendar but we must remember and pray every day for safety and health, especially of our leaders and protectors who never seem to sleep.

***

CHICKEN SOUP ON THE BARBIE? OH, VEY!!!!!

Prior in the week, Monday to be exact, I went outside at noon and quickly added tears to the environment. The skies were very gray, the fog hadn't lifted, and it was cold and damp. My brain raced into gear and the thought occurred that I should call everyone to bring winter jackets. But wait, the Jewish New Year always brings heat! Not the humid kind on the east coast where your stockings take 20 minutes to put on and your fancy clothes become limp. But hot no matter when the holiday falls to where the non-air-conditioned Temples near the beach have to rent big fans for which your temple dues will pay for somehow. So I let that thought of bad weather go away.

Our annual Jewish New Year's get together was scheduled to be at my home in the community room. My daughter Naomi and my boyfriend Harry and I were the hosts. Because of the number of family and friends that I invited and the amount of food I made and requested others to bring, the community room with an outside large patio seemed perfect. (Oy, and they all said yes!) The room on the first floor has a kitchen exactly like mine on the third floor minus everything my kitchen has. So do you get the picture that early on that morning, everything had to be schlepped downstairs in a carefully maneuvered fashion including my famous chicken soup mit matza balls?

Now add 2 type A women into my small kitchen who are in charge of "running the show". As Al Pacino said in "The scent of a Woman" – Who Chah! Just say it like it looks and forget the spelling!

So now my daughter, Naomi, has carefully coiffured my hair and tediously did my make-up, I had a real breakfast, and the show is almost ready to go on. She and I, unplanned, picked out the same color scheme for our clothing – black and white. For those of you who are not used to planning and executing a large party, take a dry run with someone who has. I have a reputation for putting on a great party and today was not going to be different.

Pots of soup, hot water pot for the matzo balls, 2 more top burners used for brisket and small savory meatballs for the kids, preheated oven for chicken, noodle kugel, large coffee pot perking with a vanilla nut roasted coffee, the large covered pool table nicely decorated with all the fall colored paper goods, ice in the chest nestled with all kinds of drinks, and THEN!!!!

A major catastrophe happens – we have no gas for the burners and the oven would only get to 215 degrees – not hot enough for anything to heat. It was now 11:00 a.m. one hour before guests would arrive. Now, if you're Jewish, you will agree with one of the worst things that can happen from a culinary standpoint is THERE WON'T BE ENOUGH TO EAT! How many cold bagels, coffee, raw veggies, and dessert can you eat? I was mortified but 2 angels appeared early – Carol and Penny who live in my building and are on the Home Owner's Board. And my long time friend Chaplain Bonnie, practiced meditation breathing and it worked! This was Saturday, it was not a gas emergency, and no one in the building knew how to fix the gas. We problem solved together and came up with using the BBQ to heat everything. And we did! All of this took over an hour but we would have hot foods that were supposed to be eaten hot. My father, may he rest in peace, always said to my mother, after he stuck his pinky in the soup – "Sara! The soup is not hot enough!" I can still hear him.

During the creation of the world, Let There Be Light resounded from the heavens. The BBQ went on with a lighter, the food was carefully again schlepped, and the guest arrived on time and understood lunch would be a little late. Harry's nephew and great nephews served the soup in special cups which warmed all of our hearts, soul, and tummies.

The most calm I experienced is when my boyfriend's brother, Manny, did the special prayers for the New Year and Shabbat. He has a cantorial voice and, with strength and perfection, sang the blessings over the wine and round raisin

filled Challah for the New Year 5771. We all sang with him and all the parts of the party started and ended on a very high note. In retrospect, we can all learn a lesson here, especially me. It's not the food that counts; it's the people that attended this New Year celebration that counts. We had Harry's family, my family, and lots of friends from various walks of life intertwining with each other. I am very blessed and thank G-D all went well. I had inner peace as soon as the prayers were being chanted. The lesson is to be thankful for what we have and not dwell on that which we didn't have. And for the relationships we have nurtured of family and friends. Maybe it takes a little negative to jar us to the positive.
And with that I say AMEN!

THE WIDOWS THREE

It is the autumn of the year
And our men died in the autumn of their years.
We three sit numbly on a bench staring at a tree.
Jane, Debbie, and Faith, me.
Why are we there and what do we see?
I, with binoculars, feel strength by looking at the wide trunk.
Debbie, with her wide brim hat, feels the warmth of the sun
through the twisted branches.
And Jane, newest of the three, sees little through her crying eyes.
We all embrace the protection of the shade,
And, with our close ties,
We will survive and thrive separately and together.

***

Glenn W. Anderson

The SWM awarded Glenn W. Anderson first prize for his short story, "Nessdahl Neavis Died Today – How Inconvenient." While a work of fiction, it illustrates that seemly insignificant souls can have uplifting stories. Glenn works in the entertainment industry as a producer, writer, and production designer. He has written works for television, a PBS special, which won an Emmy nomination, plus a BBC variety special featuring the Rolling Stones and The Beatles. He has also done rewrites on three screenplays, all of which have been produced.

For a time he taught acting and developed a systematic approach based on analyzing the performances of acclaimed and awards winning actors. He compiled his teachings into a manual for use by his students entitled "The Rudimentary Elements of the Dramatic Performance." Excerpts from this book are published online under his pen name Erik Sean McGiven.

Glenn attended several colleges including the University of Redlands, UCLA, and Cal Poly at San Luis Obispo. He studied screenwriting, music composition, engineering, and motion picture arts & sciences. He also studied acting and directing with various drama instructors.

Presently he is working on a comic western as a producer, consulting on the development of two motion picture projects, and coaching a few actors.

NESSDAHL NEAVIS DIED TODAY – HOW INCONVENIENT

Nessdahl Neavis died today, how inconvenient. He was supposed to trim Mrs. Stabler's hedges, and Carla Maursetter was counting on him to weed her garden. Other town folks had trees to prune, fences to mend, and with winter fast approaching, there were all those storm windows to install. The old handyman's death created a pesky problem for the folks of this small Midwestern town--who was going to do all these odd jobs? There were, of course, capable gardeners, painters, and carpenters in town, but who could afford them. Old man Neavis was cheap, reliable, and usually available. A kindly call to his landlady and he would normally be at your front door in the time that it took him to walk there.

Thought to be only an accommodating handyman, it would be years before the town's people came to know the true measure of this man. He lived in a walk-up at the rear of Sara Baker's house, a furnished one-room flat with a hot plate and fridge. It also had a toilet and washbasin, and that's where they found him lying on the floor, shaving soap on his face, his straight razor close by.

"A heart attack," that's what Doc Hansen called it, but in Eagan Creek other stories were being circulated. Some implied suicide, being he was such a loner. "What did he have to live for?" one person injected. Others suspected food poisoning because he hoarded food like a tenacious squirrel. But the talk kept coming back to that nagging question, whom could they get to do this work?

Some town folks resented his passing. "If he was feeling ill, he should have seen a doctor," quipped Mrs. Pratt. Arnold Lynner was equally upset by Nessdahl's death. "How inconsiderate, he should have warned us so we could have lined up someone else."

Mr. Lynner owned the prestigious home on the corner of Oak Drive and Main, the centerpiece of the community. On Sundays, churchgoers would drive by for a peek at what true wealth could buy. With its spacious lawns, wrought iron fence and manicured shrubbery, it was the envy of folks from miles around. And it was the diligent labors of Nessdahl Neavis that made it so, even though he was poorly compensated. "Work is work," he would say, "you take what's there."

The old handyman was a familiar sight in Eagan Creek. Dressed in his usual attire, faded bib overalls, a plaid flannel shirt and a sweat-stained brown fedora, folks treated him more so as an oddity than as a hired workman. Strange and aloof, he didn't fit into this tight knit community. People found him unsettling, especially those gray eyes hiding behind steel-rimmed glasses--haunting, suspicious? And the deep wrinkles in his face also left questions, maybe a vengeful and unforgiving life? Sometimes he could be abrupt and thickheaded. Yet he was a capable worker, even at seventy-one years, lean of body, hair nearly white. And somehow, he managed a meager existence, watching his pennies, working a half-day here, an hour there.

His death was most sudden. Just the day before, he had been raking leaves at the Trandahl place. High winds the night before had scattered them across the yard giving it the look of a mosaic painting, bright yellows, muted reds, on a canvas of green. Seemed a shame to disturb them, but reluctantly he did so, raking the dead foliage onto a burlap tarp. He'd fold the tarp, then deposit the leaves in a mulch pit at the rear of the property. Periodically he would mix the leaves into the decaying compost.

It was unusually warm for October, an Indian Summer sort of day. With his red handkerchief, Nessdahl wiped the perspiration from his face and neck, then the sweatband within his felt hat. He peered out at the work remaining. The job was bigger than he expected, yet if he kept at it, he could be done before lunch. Some folks would offer him a sandwich or a glass of lemonade, but the Trandahls were not one of them. Then he remembered he had some salami in the refrigerator, and the thought of a nice sandwich made the job more bearable.

When fed, he'd eat a healthy plate full and then some. He valued good cooking and a clean plate demonstrated his true appreciation. Though he rarely spoke while eating, he left the table with the same courteous words, "A good meal. Thank you ma'am." And when offered sweets or fruit, he wrapped them in a paper napkin and explained, "For later."

He wasn't finicky about what he ate, but he did have his aversions. Burnt toast was one of them. Once when Elsa Thompson served him a toasted egg sandwich, he looked at the blackened edges, then meticulously scraped the burnt portions onto his plate. Even though he consumed the sandwich, his displeasure was made known. Later, at the Women's Circle, Elsa called him an ingrate and thus another label was added to demean his already dubious character.

The fancy cooking and complex concoctions that womenfolk would toss his way also made him suspicious. How could you tell what was in it? Mashed potatoes, gravy, and a slab of meat were his true liking, and when the dish didn't suit his simple taste, he would pick through it trying to determine its contents. Harley Grooter's wife said such scrutiny insinuated she was trying to poison him. Maybe so, for she wasn't that good a cook. That's probably why Harley took most of his meals at the Roxy Café.

Children were another aversion. They and Nessdahl didn't get along and what upset him most were the tricks these youngsters would play on him. They would hide his tools or sneak up behind him and scare him. The two Benson boys were the worst of the lot and when enough became enough he turned the water hose on them. Unfortunately, they made the mistake of complaining to their father and as a result, felt the wrath of his belt.

The only youngster that Nessdahl tolerated was Emily Penske. She lived in the trailer park at the edge of town and would occasionally see him working when she came home from school. Passing by, she would survey his labors, then acknowledge his good work, nodding her head and throwing him a smile. It was a quick exchange, but nonetheless the moment stayed with him and lightened his heart.

The silent relationship continued for years until that day he was thinning out a bed of daffodils. It was a tedious job deciding which flowers should live and which should be uprooted and tossed aside. When Emily came by, she was appalled by the destruction of such lovely plants. She inquired and Nessdahl explained, "Have to give them room to grow."

"So, you're throwing these away?"

"Yeah," he shot back. Fourteen-year-old Emily had a home for these castaways and politely asked if she could have some. Nessdahl looked up at her, his eyes peering over his steel-rimmed glasses. Without any indication either way, he rose to his feet and walked away.

Emily was sure she had upset him, but then he returned carrying a burlap sack. He knelt down, put the best of the lot into the sack and handed it to her. "Here," he said. She stammered a thank you and when she walked away, a smile crept across Nessdahl's face.

As the years past the relationship grew, a nod became a wave of the hand and a hello became a short chat. And in the end, Emily Penske came to know more about old man Neavis than anyone else in town. He wasn't the crazy old kook everyone alleged him to be. And the gossip, innuendoes, and snipes were just that--nothing but talk.

But now Nessdahl Neavis was gone and his death had become an inconvenience to a great many people. Not only to those for whom he worked but also to those responsible for his transfer into the next life. The undertaker was away closing up his lake cabin, and the town's clergy deflected any obligation to this non-church member. Finally, someone mentioned they'd seen Nessdahl attending a Christmas Eve service years ago at the Lutheran Church. He sat in the balcony wearing a Macintosh jacket over his usual attire: faded bib overalls and plaid flannel shirt. Holding his stained fedora in his lap, he looked out of place, probably felt that way too. This one attendance placed the responsibility squarely on Lutheran

Pastor, Fredric Baumgartner, who incidentally was planning to get away for some midweek fishing, another inconvenience.

Nessdahl's body laid in the funeral home and with so little money to cover proper burial expenses, the coffin remained closed. What funds they found stashed in a coffee can barely covered the cheapest funeral. No one stopped by to pay their last respects, no flowers were sent, no cards of condolences, no family to grieve. Yet, when the undertaker came to put the body away, he found on top of the coffin a single yellow daffodil.

The grave was dug in the older part of the cemetery where the tombstones date back almost eighty years. A plot here was impossible to sell yet the city charged the full fee. Pastor Baumgartner and the hearse arrived, and Nessdahl Neavis was in the ground before the final words "Ashes to Ashes, Dust to Dust" were spoken. A small marker was stuck in the ground as workmen began filling in the grave.

Years past and the grave and its existence disappeared. A tractor mower had knocked over the temporary grave marker, and weeds soon engulfed this neglected resting-place. It was almost as if the man had never lived at all. It remained that way for almost seven years following his death.

Then suddenly one day a number of city workers came to this forgotten cemetery section. Weeds were cut, grass was mown and the area surveyed. Measuring carefully, they dug out a small rectangle and in it placed a wooden form held in place by stakes. Concrete was mixed, poured, and smooth with a trowel. From a wooden box, they lifted a heavy bronze marker measuring 12 by 24 inches with anchors on its underside. With precision, they pressed it into the wet concrete. It was a job well done and a tribute to the man lying below.

Whiffs of snow clung to the plague's raised letters, frosting the brown grass, capping tombstones. It was now November, bitterly cold, trees barren. A yellow school bus made its way up the twisting cemetery road coming to a stop near the older section. Stepping off the bus, a young woman helped her third grade students disembark. A high school student trailed and moved away in the opposite direction carrying a black case. Bundled up, the children clustered around their teacher then followed her in a reverent procession.

They gathered around his grave and looked at the shiny bronze marker. The teacher began, "This is where Nessdahl Neavis is buried, a soldier, a hero, and my friend." She recapped the man's life, his service in World War One, his recovery in an Army hospital, and the subsequent lose of his wife and child to the Spanish flu. She talked about his struggles, about the many places he traveled to find work during the Great Depression. He was a neglected soul she said, overlooked and often maligned. Even his own community failed to recognize his service and achievements. But one determined soul dug deep to discover the truth.

And while the bronze marker indicated the start and end of his life, there is another life that goes on. One that lives in the hearts and memories of those he left behind. This was her lesson, a lesson about honor, respect, and human kindness. And through the coming school year, these young children would come to know this man as well as their teacher, Emily Penske.

She gave each student a small American Flag and instructions to place it in the ground next to the grave marker. Off in the distance, the sound of "Taps" echoed through the cemetery as each child took its turn. Seventeen flags fluttered in the wind, a fitting tribute to this soldier for tomorrow was November 11th, Armistice Day. When they were done, Emily pulled from her purse and placed on the grave a yellow daffodil.

They stood there in silence, feeling the loss, yet savoring the moment that would shape the rest of their lives. Before leaving, they gazed once more at the bronze marker: "Cpl. Nessdahl W. Neavis, April 3rd 1891 - October 27th 1962, U.S. Army, WW1 1918 France." Below were emblems indicating awards for his distinguished military service: Two Purple Hearts, a Silver Star, and The Congressional Medal of Honor.

Ian Gordon

AKA

Jan Perry Van Gordon

Ian Gordon was interested in science, technology and science fiction at a very early age. Experimenting with chemistry and rockets, he was once chased out of the regular science section of a library because a librarian thought that it was too "adult."

Exploring the fields of chemistry and basic electricity, he won a scholarship to a correspondence school in electronics.

After high school, he found himself working in the aerospace field.

During the seventies, he became involved with the then new field of micro-computing, joining and starting clubs, classes and building one of the first kit computers, long before Apple.

He explored that career in civilian jobs, working in computer stores, support agencies and even a toy design group. He started his own business in the computer field.

Retiring, he now does newsletter work and web design for several local clubs.

ALICE MOVING UNDER SKIES

Still she haunts me, phantomwise.
Alice moving under skies
Never seen by waking eyes...

...In a Wonderland they lie,
Dreaming as the days go by,
Dreaming as the summers die:

Ever drifting down the stream--
Lingering in the golden gleam--
Life, what is it but a dream?

I sat in one of the few 1950's style diners left on the Coast and satisfied myself with an almost perfect burger... and a real ice cream soda.

It was luxury.

The waitress came up and said, “Enjoy your poison, Frenchy?”

“It’s great, but...”

“Why so glum, Sam?”

“Well, I haven’t had any new cases lately.” I complained, “It’s not so bad, I still get paid by the boys with cigars, but I’m just treadin’ water. I’d like to be doin’ something.”

“Bored, then?”

“Yeah, I guess... but I have this feelin’ there’s somethin’... something coming.”

“Train?” she kidded, “Deer in the headlights?”

“Close.” I snorted, “Might be good... might be dangerous... dunno.”

“And it might be good and dangerous... Well, enjoy, Sam.” she said, waltzing away.

She’s a good muff, but doesn’t understand.

That made me think of Sally, a part-time girlfriend I knew that seemed to understand... me... sometimes.

I went cross-town to my flat, a shared co-ed place with all the amenities. Now with the boys with cigars paying me, I could afford it. I even had enough to get my old Studebaker fixed.

Sally was in, she was reading.

"Hey, Frenchy," she greeted me, "Yotta see this... some great stories... seem so real!"

I remembered the reality tri-vid shows ten years ago... they sucked eggs. "You sure?"

"No, really." she went on, "It's almost like someone you know."

She read me a few pages. Seemed pretty good.

"Who pubs this stuff?" I borrowed the Sho-Tablet® , scolled down to the credits.

"Dreamtime Publishers" it read, "Sea-Tac"

"Hmm, West Coast." I was interested.

"Can you sub me for more?" she asked.

"Sure, just use my cred-scan." I'm generous.

I got a call... someone I knew. He said, "Meet at one, okay?"

"Okay." I repeated, then clicked off.

"Girlfriend?" she asked, not too jealously.

"Nope." I answered. She knew I meant it.

"Business, then." she concluded, "Well, good luck!"

She hugged, I left.

"Okay," I said, seating myself in an out-of-the way bar mid-city... "Wassup?"

It was a quiet, unassuming meeting place for a slightly sloppy race-track looking guy and a slightly shabby-looking businessman.

"Strange business." the business-type said, leaning closer.

No one was listening... no one would care.

It was the kind of place where everybody kept to themselves.

That's the way he liked it.

"C'mon." I urged.

"It's... this 'Dreamtime" stuff," he said, leaning closer, "heard of it?"

"Yep... so?"

"Dunno... something's going on... the main... office..."

"Yeah," I completed his thought, "... wants to know."

"That's it." he coughed.

"So..." I asked, "Why not you? You're an U/C agent."

He looked around, "Can't... I'd stick out. Cover blown."

He slipped me a packet. I snuck a peek.

Fake ID's... Good job, looked worn and used.

And, moolah... cred sticks and real cash.

I didn't need the money, but these looked unlimited.

"So much!" I said, he shushed me.

"More when..."

"Where should I start?" I asked, knowing the answer.

"Saint... Glover Street."

I caught the next maglev North to Sea-Tac.

Almost fell asleep... woulda gone up and through the Aleutian Chunnel... ended up in China.

I shuddered. Good job the station bell woke me up.

Found Glover. Small office, sniffed around... buncha desks with 'puters and Sho-Tabs.

Didn't look like a pub house. Girl came up, I said I was an author, asked about work.

"No," the sec said, smiling inwardly, "we... uh... have our own... sources."

Waited til late, snuck around back.

It's a good thing to look like a sloppy tout.

Bum crawled out, holding up a moldy sandwich.

"I can share..." he said, looking a little afraid.

"Not hungry." I said.

He shambled away, "... everybody's hungry..." he mumbled.

"Curse paperless offices!" I thought.

Wasn't much there, surprised it wasn't locked. Most dustbins are these days.

Found a 'gram sheet and a shipping label that stood out.

Both had a name... "Nor-Ways Legal" That was all.

Went to the tube station, got in a comm cubicle.

"Nor-Ways" came up on the screen... several addresses.

"We take care of your trust needs, wills and deeds. All legal resources." it said.

Nearby address, only four stops from Dreamtime.

Cleaned up a little in a minitel, got some sleep.

In the morning, went to the Nor-Ways office on Stanton.

Fished through my ID's, found the right ones.

Went in. Gorgeous, up-tight muff met me.

"How can we serve you, Sir?"

Told her I was a dick... well... I used the term, "Private Investigator."

Said that I was looking for more permanent work.

She said, "Of course. Nor-Ways is always looking for competent legal help."

Showed me some forms. Filled them out, talked to ER person.

She checked me out, I checked her out.

"Everything looks good." she said, sitting down again.

"How long do I..." I started to ask.

"You can start tomorrow." she said.

"Don't you have a waiting list?" I asked.

"Not too many professionals come here." she said, "Most go to our LA office."

"Oh..." I mused, "So... what kind of things will I..."

"Well," she said, "that's up to our Trust Director... we have a need there."

Called him that night, "In…" I said, "Nor-Ways."

"That's a strange connection." he replied, "This gets weirder and weirder."

"That's all now." I said, "Pub house... trust company... you figure."

"No, you figure. Lemme know." he said, clicking off.

As far as I could tell in the few weeks, the trust company did exactly that... all kinds of legal services.

But, something finally clicked. I talked to a client.

"What's this?" he said, "Identity Rights...?"

I replied, "Yes, the ID Protection Act that was passed a few years ago, allows an individual's identity information to become public domain upon his demise. Of course, this can be amended on appeal, but very few people care. It also protects from ID theft because if it's public domain, no one can misuse it."

"What exactly do you mean?" he continued to query, "Cred info? Stocks?"

I answered exactly as they had taught me, "No... of course not. All financial bonds and information default directly to the immediate family or agent. No, this refers only to the client's history and personal details... and, of course, names and direct identity are made anonymous."

"So," he persisted, "someone could read all about my... or his life, but wouldn't know who it was."

"That's right," I said, "just like the recent census info, no one would know who it was."

Then it hit me!

I concluded my business with this client and thought for a while.

I went to a local pub to think a little deeper.

Somebody sat down across from me... he looked familiar.

"I can share..." he said.

Cleaned up, this was the bum from the rubbish bin.

"Not hungry." I said.

"... everybody's hungry..." he said.

"Who you working for?" I asked.

"I'd have to kill you." we both said, and laughed.

I knew then that he was an agent for the other group.

Both agencies compete with each other, but rarely share information.

"I'm an independent." I said. This seemed to make him more comfortable.

"Look," he said, "I saw you at Nor-Ways... figured out the connection to Dreamtime?"

"Not quite." I said, "But something weird is going on."

"That's for sure." he agreed.

We looked at each other for a while...

"Dreamtime is pubbing in China." he offered.

I threw him a bone, "It has something to do with the ID Protection Act... I think."

"Mmmm." he puzzled, "Makes sense... public domain... yes..."

"I think so, to." I agreed.

"I think if I cleaned up, I may get an in with Dreamtime." he said.

I said, "Tried that, not taking writers."

He laughed, "Do I look like a writer? No... I mean... services."

I laughed, "Well, if you have to clean up to look like a janitor."

He laughed, too, "I can look like the President or CEO if I have to, but I'm more comfortable bumming around."

I paid the tab with the promise of more exchanges. We left separately.

I called my man, gave him the story.

"Other agency, hmmm." he sounded worried, "Fair exchange?"

"Got more than I gave." I said, "We both had the gist of it."

"So... Nor-Ways... Dreamtime... China, huh?"

"No," I remanded, "Nor-Ways... China... Dreamtime... China... public distribution. I think the info is laundered through China before going to Dreamtime."

"So..." he pondered, "It's getting complicated."

"Yes." I agreed, "Probably more so than we know. I'll check the comm recs."

Clicked off and scrambled codes again. I had the code list in my packet.

I'm getting lazy in my old age. Snuck a sniffer in the comm closet at work.

Bought an enhanced Sho-Tab with keyboard and hacking aps.

Back at my hovel, I could watch the comm hash at my leisure.

There was an ebbing of the squawking at the end of the day... but...

Just about midnight, the hash-board lit up... Someone was working late.

About half was Chinese... with a little Korean... clicked on my Unicode.

"Very interesting!" I thought... linking the datastream to my agent's coded input.

"Did exactly the same thing." my bum friend said, as we sipped in our fave pub.

"Chinese and Korean connection?" I nudged.

"Yep," he said, "Both ways."

"But," said my agent, "what are they doing that's illegal. That info can be accessed by anyone, it's all public."

"Well, how about the restrictions?"

"That's tricky. Our embassies are right now making arrangements to open up information both ways."

"So," I said, "it's a political football."

"In spades!" he said, "Obviously Dreamtime was aware of that."

"But, they have to have been planning this for some time."

"Yes..." sounding hopeful, "but... it's still tricky."

I was still suspicious, I had found another connection in the datastream.

There was a mortuary company, with offices all over.

Went to a local one and broke in at night.

There didn't seem to be any security... perhaps they felt secure in their obscurity.

I found a lab, hidden in the depths. My clue was the tire marks leading to a cement wall.

Found my way in through the air system.

Flashlight in hand, found myself surrounded by bodies.

Every one was hooked up to some kind of 'puter, with a lot of wires.

I knew what it was, I've heard of the latest science on brain waves and what happens to our dream and thoughts when we pass away.

They were harvesting the last, dying thoughts and dreams of recently dead people!

I had suspected something like this, but had no idea it was connected to Dreamtime.

This beats the bag and tag boys all hollow!

According to what I found out about psychs and other personal services selling their records under the table to a closet agency that was connected through the Korean underground to Dreamtime, it all came together!

Back at the pub, my agent, my bum friend and I were having an ale... and a laugh.

So, we concluded, the conniving companies, both local and Oriental, were crying over their gold bars while the politicians were scratching their collective heads... and the reading public didn't have a clue.

"Someone could break the story." my bum friend said.

"And we'd have to kill them!" we laughed.

Two weeks later, the story broke; "American company stealing people's dreams and selling them to the Koreans!" it read. They didn't have it right... but they never do.

My agent said it was my bum friend, but I think it was one of the ladies at Nor-Ways... or Dreamtime... unless somebody hacked my datastream link.

After all, news agencies are the third estate.

Then, Alice moving under skies
Her never seeing by waking eyes,
Ever dreaming as the days go by,

Ever dreaming as the summers die,
Now drifting down the stream,
Dreaming life, what is it but a dream?

HOUNDERWOCKY

`Twas twilight, and the slimy fog
Did curl and roll around the tor:
All gloomy were the moor ponies,
And the bitterns booming on the moor.

"Beware the Hound of Hell, my friend!
The paws that pounce, the jaws that bite!
Beware the Selden bird, my friend,
The Notting Hill Assassin is alight!"

He took his Penang stick in hand:
Long time the canine foe he sought --
So rested he by the grey stone hut,
And stayed awhile in thought.

And, while in careful thought he stood,
The Hellish Hound, with eyes of fire,
Came moaning through the foggy wood,
And creeping through the mire!

One, two! One, two! And thus and so,
His pistol hand went Crack! and Crack!
He left it dead, and with his friends
He went, triumphant, back.

"And, has thou slain the "Hound of Hell?"
Come to my mansion, my friends all!
O glorious day! Hallooh! Halloa!'
They reveled in the hall.

'Twas twilight, and the slimy fog
Did curl and roll around the tor:
All gloomy were the moor ponies,
And the bitterns booming on the moor.

Ildy Lee

International author, poet, songwriter, and editor of this anthology, Ildy Lee writes in three languages. She studied law at the Paris Sorbonne where her father was a professor. Her articles appeared in the L.A. Times, the Daily Breeze, the Peninsula News and many international publications. Winner of the Torrance Shakespeare Poetry Competition twice, she is also the 2012 President of the Southwest Manuscripters.

Born In Hungary, Ildy survived the communist regime as a child. Granddaughter of a classical French composer, she is related to Zilahy, the "Hungarian Hemmingway." Persecuted by the regime, her family exiled to Paris where the destitute refugee girl dressed in oversized clothes from the Salvation Army rose to musical stardom as a recording artist. Her life is a Cinderella story: Romance with a royal prince, first kiss from Salvador Dali, General De Gaulle's invitation to the Paris opera, TV shows, etc…

Anchored now in the safe harbor of her ocean side home, Ildy inspires and motivates others. Her song "Blind Guitarist" built a home for blind children, her "David" raised money on the Jerry Lewis telethon, and her "Old Man's Legacy" is helping the homeless. Besides charity work, Ildy Lee is known as the owner-designer of the original "Dream Home," the Palos Verdes Art Center's media sensation that raised over a million dollars to benefit the community. Ildy Lee's latest project is "Perilous Journey," a book about her fascinating life. Ms. Lee writes, directs and produces films at her Multimedia Studios. For more, tune into her website: **www.ildylee.com** or check out her fascinating videos at ***www.YouTube.com/ildylee***

MOON OVER VENICE

Shakespeare Award winner poem (2010)

Venice is seductive at night
Rising naked from the waters
Like Botticelli's Venus.
Sensuous bride
Of the Adriatic Sea,
Her teasing caresses are
Caught in the silver net
Of the full moon
Her ghostly beauty emerges
From the murky waters
As I glide in silent gondolas
Without you now.

The stretched-out white bridges,
Silken thighs of her sculpted body,
Arch over to caress the canals.
The moonlit cups of round cupolas
Are her marble nipples in erection.
The gondolier lets me off.
I breath the magic and walk alone.
Slender poles are jutting out
From the water, echoing my hollow footsteps,
They keep me company. The muffled thud of empty boats
Clash like we used to clash, one against the other,
In morbid harmony.

As raindrops wet
The shiny cobblestones
Venice is even more beautiful
In her sadness
She is a mourning widow
Wailed in black nostalgia
Fragile like an abandoned child,
Seductive as a somber sonata.
The shimmering lights
Still tremble on the water
Gloomy clouds obscure the moon.
Mist swallows
The palace of the Doges
That looms like a ghost ship
Near the dark lagoon.

Suddenly I understand
How small my world has been
In search of new frontiers
While Venice is awaiting its fate
Sitting on death-row.
These bridges, palaces and
gondoliers
Are but future marble graves
Like your memories,
This city with all its treasures
Sometimes soon will sink beneath the waves…

Dress Rehearsal

(Shakespeare Award winner poem (2012)

Ferocious fortress from Medieval times
Bryce Canyon's blood-soaked cliffs
Are soaring cathedrals
On a vast unearthly stage
Fantasy-induced phantoms
Twisted into eerie peaks
In purple glow.

You, soundless inhabitants,
Wind sculpted spires
And towering pinnacles
Of this petrified Metropolis,
What have you done
To deserve such curse?

The silent limestone sculptures
Echoing my footsteps
Have no speaking parts.
Gleaming like fragments
Of broken bones,
They're reminders
Of fallen warriors.

Looming amongst mute statues
Immobile actors are staged
For Greek tragedies.

A pale Delphic Oracle in toga
Laments in nature's amphitheater
Frozen in time
Awaiting another ice age.

Whitewashed cliff walls
Are stone curtains
Bathed in the harsh stage light
Of the setting sun.
Blinded, dwarfed,
Heart hammering,
I forgot my monologue!

Solitary actor
In God's amphitheater
I stare into the eye
Of a black wolf:
My audience!

FREEDOM

Freedom frightens me
Almost as much as oppression.
When out of control, this monster
Can freely breed violence and crime
Knowing it's sheltered by the Constitution.
Even though war zones have moved to the
Decaying belly of inner cities,
Bullets can hit anyone anywhere,
On the freeway, in our bedrooms, at the movies.
So, we hide in our homes,
Self imposed prisoners

Held hostages by fear:
Fear of being freed from our possessions,
Freed from our loved ones,
Freed from our fragile lives.
Caught in so many wars
Peace is now a politically incorrect word
And safety is...utopia!
Too much freedom is just as bad as not enough.
In my country we yearned for freedom
We broke our chains and risked our life to see its face
But here in the free world I found confusion instead:
Freedom-chaos from lack of enforcing the rules
In a permissive world that flirts with Anarchy
The face of freedom is but melting wax
Under the white mask of death
Stained by the warm blood of
Massacred school children
Mowed down in their innocence
By the scythes of permissive freedom.
Here everyone can buy a gun and
Gun down everyone he pleases.
(Even Presidents.)
They call it freedom.
I don't!
I can't...
I wont!

JUSTICE,

Blindfolded for centuries
Take off your scarf,
And face the truth.
The world has changed
Since you fell asleep.
Now dog eats dog and
Man sues man.
Here is the new bible:
If you are clumsy and fall
On the floor, in a store,

Sue the city, sue the state,
Sue your doctor, sue your best friends,
And sue the store!
Today crime pays. It pays well.
The bigger the crime, the bigger the pay.
Felons get awarded millions
When injured on the job:
While robbing or killing!
The cop who dares to interfere with the lawbreaker,
And God forbid, injure the poor thief or murderer
Will be brought to justice.
The OJ Simpsons
Get away with murder.
A skilled murderer gets to write a book.
The media makes him an instant hero
And Hollywood opens its arms and rewards him
With a film.
The guilty are glorified
The innocent are pushed under the carpet
Nobody wants to hear their boring story!

So, Justice, take off your scarf
And wake up.
You can't afford to be blind anymore.
And neither can we!

FEAR…AND PREJUDICE

Fear often stops us from being fair.

I caught the last metro in Paris
Lonely late voyagers,
Smelly beggars
Drunks laying in their vomit.
Dimly lit corridors
Littered with trash
At Gare du Nord
I ran to catch the last train

To my banlieu-suburb
The smoke-filled compartments
Are chocked with unwashed body odor.
Men…Nothing but men!
Dark skinned men from Africa
And curly haired Muslims from Algeria.
Poverty is sticking to their fake leather jackets,
To their greasy hair and musty underwear.
Tired and defeated,
These are desperate men
Rejected by society
Their defying glances shaped
By shattered dreams
And broken promises.
Men, seduced and lured by the city of lights
Yet abandoned to the city of darkness.
Bored, they turn to the
Only lonely female: me!
Probing, hungry eyes are
Stripping me naked.
Looking at the floor
I hear their heavy breathing.
Some giggle, some whistle
Some use obscene gestures
To impress their peers.

I tuck my long blond hair
Under my winter coat,
Defenseless lamb amongst
A pack of macho wolfs.

***

Two A.M.
At the deserted train station
Of my hometown destination.
A large black man followed me from the train.
Was his oversized duffle bag hiding a shotgun?
A Riffle? A homemade bomb, or his rage?
Echoing footsteps, heartbeat, panic!

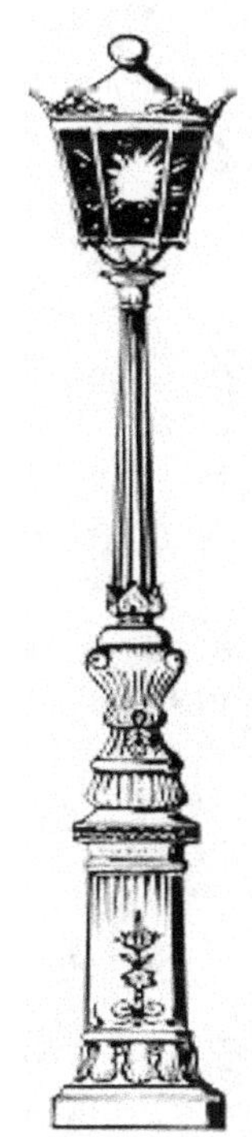

I slowed down, he did the same.
I hastened my steps. So did he.
I ran.
He caught up with me!
In the halo of a streetlamp
He reached for my bag.

I wanted to scream
"Take everything, just don't hurt me!"
But my mouth couldn't form the words.

The towering black man,
Reached for my bags
As his ultimate shadow blocked out the light
Overhead.
Then said in a soft voice:
"These are too heavy for a small woman like you.
Let me carry them for you!"

For a twenty-minute walk home
I learned about his country
The struggle of his people
To fight hunger, to say alive.
I learned about his two jobs,
The night classes in college,
And his hope to bring his sick mother
To France one day

At the corner of my street
We said goodbye.
I watched him fade into darkness,
The same darkness that is slowly
Swallowing his dreams, one by one,
Along with our prejudice.
I wanted to run after him
To hug him and hold him
For this man who had frightened me so much
Had just restored my faith in human kindness.

Plumbers Versus Doctors?

Whatever happened to the Hippocratic Oath?

One evening I experienced some alarming symptoms. I placed an emergency call to my doctor's office. But the doctor on call answered all my questions by "I don't know!" I said: If a trained Physician doesn't know, then who will?

"*All I can tell you* - he said- *either come to my office tomorrow, or go to an emergency room now.*" This was not the kind of help I expected. My plumber could have told me as much. *Thank you very much* - I replied - *but the reason I am calling you is to get your professional insight in making this decision. Are my symptoms severe enough, Doctor, to require immediate medical attention, yes or no?*

"That's a choice you have to make on your own" he grunted. *Based on what?* - I asked. - *I am not a trained physician, you are! "But I don't know your medical history, lady." It's not about my medical history, Doctor, it's about my immediate symptoms. What am I supposed to do? Go to an ER or wait to see you tomorrow? "I already gave you your choices. I have another call. Good by." - Clank!*

If doctors won't help, than who will? Suddenly it dawned on me: Of course, I should have called the plumber! Let's face it, they both charge the same, they both are unable to provide medical advise, but at least the plumber is kind, helpful and supportive.

And that is, in itself, healing!

21 Century Artist.

As a writer, my tools are no longer paper and pen but spread sheets, fax machines and computer printouts.

As a composer, my instruments are no longer piano and guitar, but samplers, synthesizers and midi stations.

As an artist, my media is no longer in oils or watercolor. My palette is a laser printer, my brushes are color scanners, my eyes are digital cameras, my canvas is a flat monitor, and my gallery to exhibit is the internet!

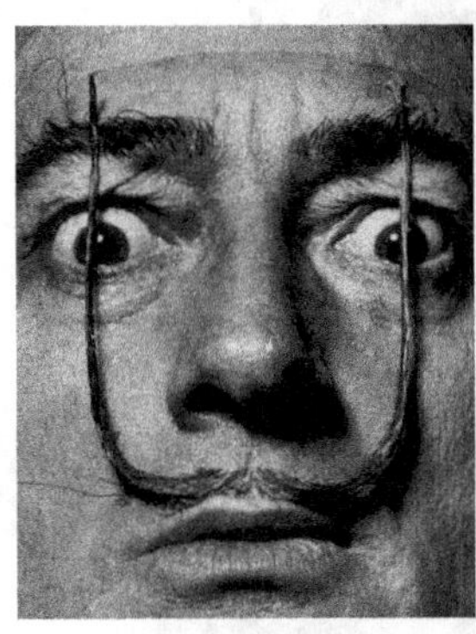

Ray's Sweet Kiss

Salvador Dalí gave me my first kiss
But I can assure you that it wasn't bliss.
I was just a schoolgirl, innocent and pure
I thought he'll protect me, for I felt insecure.

As we said goodbye, I extended my hand
But he grabbed me instead! - I did not understand.
Then he forced his thick lips over mine, the pervert
His curled-up mustache was hard, poking me, and it hurt.

He happened to be Ray Bradbury's friend.
Why did he act this way? I could not comprehend.
When many years later, I told the story to Ray,
He laughed so hard that he spilled his café-au-lait.

And before we parted, his fans could take a peek
As Ray deposited a light kiss on my cheek.
A goodbye kiss so tender, not an act of folly,
Much sweeter than the one from Salvador Dalí

Since this Anthology is dedicated to Ray Bradbury's memory, let me share with you the preface of my upcoming poetry book:

Summer in Italy

This poetry book is dedicated to

Ray Bradbury,

whose soaring talent and creative imagination paired with hard work, tenacity and determination raised him to a legendary status throughout the world.

Mr. Bradbury, thank you for sharing with us, Southwest Manuscripters, your knowledge, your passion to write and your love for life, for over 55 years. Your yearly contribution to us, struggling or budding writers, is not only a testimony to your loyalty and generosity but it also encourages us to reach our fullest potential. Your seminars motivate us to move the world! How can we not share our success with you when you help us to reach it through your invaluable insights!

Thank you for the inspiration:
Ildy Lee

Check out *"Ray Bradbury, An Intimate Tribute"* on YouTube:
http://youtu.be/w0K-dmZJHT8

Janis Albright Lukstein

Janis Albright Lukstein loved hearing Ray Bradbury's wonderful stories and has been inspired to write by the Southwest Manuscripters' literary speakers and articles in their newsletter. Her father Scott Albright wrote poetry for his family; so Janis started to write as well. She earned her English teaching credential in 1970 from Cal State University, Long Beach and taught English and drama at a local middle school for over forty years. After being a Caring Hospital Clown, she is now a clown with the Classic Clowns of Whittier.

Janis' recent poetry selections include rhyming poetry written after becoming a Laughter leader with Laughter-*YogaAmerica.com* and leading workshops sharing "The Health Benefits of Laughter" at the *CancerSupportRedondoBeach.org* where she is "Tickled Pink," a volunteer clown. At the annual Cowboy Poetry and Music Festival by the Palos Verdes Peninsula Horsemen's Association, each January Janis performs sing-a-long and family horse experience poems.

Janis is a member of the SoCalHaikuStudyGroup and her haikus are published in their annual anthology. With Kathy Wilson's Poets on Site, Janis writes ekphrastic poetry inspired by contemporary or antique art like in the haiku "eroded sacred rock." You can contact Janis at ***Calkeypals@aol.com.***

studying haiku~
waves of emotion~~
~ebb and flow~~~

Janis Lukstein

eroded sacred rock-
looking through life
framed by holes

sharing the candle light—
offering to take my photo
pilgrim lives her prayer

LAUGH WITH TICKLED PINK

Laughter is a great way to go
Norman cousins said it was so!
Comedy video “Ha’s” did swell
to help him become very well

“Wonderful; amazing!” say some
Just say, “HA, HA” for lots of fun
Follow these directions:
“Ho, ho, ha, ha, haaaaa”

Laughter Yoga is a way of life
With “ha, ha, haaa’s” there is no strife
Laugh with joy at the rising sun
“Ha, ha” at daily things to have fun

Laugh at yourself doing a flip
Laugh as your lover kisses your lip
Laugh at ‘most every thing “in the sun”
Laugh “ha, ha” so we all can be “one”

OUR HEALING GARDEN

Nancy worked to give life to unused space
now transformed to a healing garden place
where sunlight shines there to make us all well
in peaceful harmony our spirits do swell

"A Healing Garden for one and all!"
That is our Wellness Community's call
Our flowers are here to see and smell
helping us to smile and feel truly well

Some years ago volunteers made it our own
where two squirrels love to play and call home
One even came inside to check out our room
so Tom chatted with her; then out she zoomed

A ruby throated humming bird with a long bill
hovers by the fountain's flowing water to get his fill
******Flash of ******red******oh so bright*****
We knew our experience was pure delight

Wellness is our community's mission for life
We meditate and pray to relieve our strife
Relaxed and refreshed we do feel the call
for Laughter Yoga to bring joy and love to all

So when a towhee calls you for a date,
listen and please come to rejuvenate!

UNDER THE RAINBOW IN THE HEALING GARDEN

Tickled Pink is holding the pen
A pen to write -- we don't know why
as we sit on pillows,
we learn to - - -f-l-y - - ----

To our delight, there comes a squirrel
we don't know- but we call it Burl
We throw him bread
and he seems well-fed :-)

Crows, finches'n'house sparrows galore
We're straight-outdoors -- never a bore
"Hey, it's almost one!"
"But we're not quite done...."

"Too much to do," says Chemo Brain
"Your eyes are so sleepy... Ehh-just strain..."
"Be Happy- Don't Worry'n'Just listen
to the warbler's sweet refrain."

sweeter-sweeter-sweeter, sugar-sugar

sweeter-sweeter-sweeter, sugar-sugar

sweeter, sugar-sugar . . .

A PROPOSAL

I must get up to muck the wooden floor
the menial household task begs to be done
to make the gruel for you whom I adore
to be patient I'll not bake in the sun

My wish is not to clean another house
to be nurtured like you from time of birth
cultured lady . . . nay a simpleton mouse
to labor in pain; give me love and worth

to escape to your gardens in the South of France
to taste sweet meats and fruit cured in honey;
as your wife, I will love the contra dance
to leap into your bed full of money
to share our joy in married life today
so let us tarry longer- then be away!

1942 LOVE LETTERS

Dear Beautiful Irene,

Thank you, Darling for your wonderful letters
during this time we're apart, my precious pigeon,
I mopped the floors today, got five hours' sleep
standing guard duty last night- 3,000 miles away
is too far for us to see each other and so I am saving
my days for after officers' training

Studying all the time for exams plus inspecting my
platoon at roll call- had to get after some sloppy guys.
Don't worry Sweetheart- you're perfect

Dennis Floyd Albright is a great name; my dad
would be proud of his namesake. Hope you are
feeling well; we both will be due soon. . .
I will finally come home and our son will be born.

Our sweetness will never die.
Hugs and kisses forever my love,

Scotty

THE WIFE'S CALL

Weeping Woman's familiar with The Wall
She has crawled up huge steps at Badaling
She has traveled to meet her true wife's call

She has seen the long side wall shadows cling
She has touched rough stones of the great divide
She has heard suffering by Emperor Ming:

seen the wall with her husband still inside
bartered with royalty who wanted to know
how this young beauty opened the wall wide
with powerful faith and love as pure snow—
her cherished husband heaven she did send
No bow to ruler but plan to bestow a burial
jumped off the cliff to begin
a life with him on their Chinese dragon~~~

***

ONLY YESTERDAY

only yesterday,

I held your hand

in dreams covered

with cherry blossoms

still remembered

SEASONS OF HAIKU

pink cherry blossoms
cloud the sky—
dreamer

hot air balloons—
colorful quilts
rise to the sun

the Rose Parade—
music wakens me
to the New Year

row of flags
by row of graves—
price of freedom

mountains—
floating heavenly
among the clouds

spring buds—
ready to explode life
from dormant tree

golden-orange
leaves falling—
church bells

orange and black koi
fan dancing—
waterfall

five hundred ducks—
circle to roost
in the wet meadow

terracotta warriors—
restored life savers
still stand guard

orange dragon fly
balances on tulle—
sunset

dancing magnolia—
pink petals lined
in white for modesty

purple blossoms
rain on my head—
jacaranda

no consideration
for stargazers—
the full moon

natal journey ends
with first breath—
birth

golden poppies
open to the sun—
Mother's Day

seeks body for
fulfillment—
Chinese robe

lupine seeds
already dispersed—
empty pods

naked lily stalks—
pirate swords
for neighborhood kids

invitation to listen—
pebbles tumble in waves
at Hidden Cove

Jeri Fonté

It wasn't until I had a story I felt I wanted and needed to tell that I became a writer. It evolved out of a serendipitous visit to Uganda in 1971. Following a safari in Kenya and Tanzania, my traveling companion and I considered going to Mombasa. But elephants had torn up the water lines into town, so we went to Uganda instead. It was there that I found the Africa of my dreams. Later, when hearing of the atrocities committed by the Idi Amin regime, a story took shape in my mind of two families affected by those events. It became the novel *The Lure of the Lion* (*TLTL*).

Wanting to avoid the automatic rejection process when submitting to established publishers, I decided to independently publish *TLTL*. At the suggestion of a fellow SWM member, Varda Murrell, I chose Xlibris. *TLTL* has received good reviews, and is now available as an e-book, as well as in hard-cover and paperback.

Africa presented another story when in 1994/95, while researching *TLTL*, my two then-teenaged sons and I met a young Somali refugee in Nairobi. I wrote the account of his life and coming to America as an asylum seeker in a screenplay titled *Matatu to the Moon*. It was a semifinalist in the Nicholl Competition, sponsored by The Academy of Motion Picture Arts and Sciences, being recognized as one of the best 100 scripts out of almost 4200 submitted that year.

LONDON, TWAIN, AND MISTER PAYNE

This short story was a first place winner in a SWM contest. It was inspired by a visit to Samuel Clemens' home in Connecticut.

He was four years old again. Nestled on his mother's lap, he caressed her soft ivory dress, its color contrasting with her ebony skin. His head resting upon her breast, he could feel the vibrations of her voice. She was reading from a book that was as familiar to him as the sound of her breathing. But the words he heard were not the words in the book. Nor could he hear in them the sound of his mother's voice. Suddenly the harsh ring of a bell swept the image from his mind. He heard chairs being scraped across the floor, accompanied by children's excited voices.

"Davey? Davey, wake up."

Davey lifted his head from the desk. All his fifth-grade classmates had left. Only his teacher, Miss Bouchard, remained.

"Davey, it's time to go home," she told him gently. It was her voice Davey had heard in his dream. "Don't forget, book reports are due next Friday."

Davey nodded absently as he gathered his belongings.

"If you'd like, I could arrange for a tutor from the high school to help with your reading."

"Okay, Miss Bouchard," he agreed half-heartedly as he turned to leave.

"Have a good weekend," she offered with forced cheerfulness. The slope of his shoulders gave her the impression that he carried the weight of the world on his ten-year-old back.

Davey hadn't gone far from school when a scraggly-looking little dog ran up to him with wagging tail and a happy grin. As Davey bent down to pet it, it licked his face excitedly.

"Mister Thornton!" a stern voice addressed the little animal. "Where are your manners?"

Davey glanced up into the kind eyes of an old man with snow-white hair and a thin, white mustache set on his wrinkled black face. It was a gentle, caring face.

"I apologize for my companion," the old man stated.

"No bother. Whadya call 'im?"

"Mister Thornton. Mister Buck Thornton. And I am Mister Augustus Payne. You may call me Gus."

Davey rose and shook Gus' extended hand. "Davey LeBeaux," he offered shyly.

"Bless my soul! You are the young man I was looking for!"

Davey gave him a quizzical look as the old man continued. "You are the Davey LeBeaux whose teacher has inquired about a tutor, are you not?"

Davey responded with a nod.

"Then I am here to be of assistance," Gus told him with a slight bow. He removed a slim book from the pocket of his coat. "I brought something which might be of interest to you. It is a book I enjoyed reading when I was your age. It concerns a dog. From your rapport with Mister Thornton, I see you are a young man who cares for dogs."

"Yeah, but I've never had one," Davey admitted sadly. "So, what's the book?"

"It was written by the author Jack London. Perhaps you are familiar with his work?"

Davey shook his head as he took the aged volume from Gus' outstretched hand.

"Jack London was a great adventure writer," Gus informed him. "This particular story takes place in Alaska, during the Gold Rush. It is titled *The Call of the Wild*. Perhaps, if you are not in a hurry, we could start on it now?"

"I guess," Davey answered.

"We had better notify your parents that you will be home a little late."

"That's okay. My dad works late."

"And your mother?"

"My ma's gone," Davey shot back with surprising anger. "She left us."

Gus studied him with compassion. "Why don't we sit over there and take turns reading?"

Davey and Mister Thornton followed Gus to a bench where a tall sycamore tree shaded them from the warm Louisiana sun. Gus began aloud: "Buck did not read the newspapers --" the little dog picked up his ears and cocked his head at the mention of his name.

"'Buck'?" Davey asked. "Is that where he got his name?"

Gus nodded as he began again. When he read the description of the Buck in the story, Davey grinned. "Don't sound nothin' like your Buck," he commented.

Gus smiled in agreement while handing Davey the book. The boy started haltingly as he began where Gus left off. Soon he fell into the rhythm of the story, and his words flowed freely.

"You read extremely well," Gus complimented him when they reached the end of the chapter. "Perhaps your parents have helped you?"

"My dad can't read too well," Davey offered thoughtfully. "He's good with numbers, but he says words seem to jump around the page."

Gus nodded knowingly before glancing at his pocket watch. "Dear me, it's nearing five o'clock."

As they rose to leave, Davey handed him the book. "Take it with you," Gus told him. "Perhaps we could resume reading tomorrow? Unless you and your father --"

"My dad works Saturdays," Davey interrupted.

"If you'd like, and if it's all right with him, we could meet here around ten?"

"Okay, Mister Payne."

"Gus," the kind old man reminded him.

"Gus," Davey repeated softly as he petted Mister Thornton good-bye.

For the first time in months, Davey hurried home, excited to continue reading the tale of the magnificent dog. But when he read the part where the devoted animal realizes his master is dead, anger rose in the boy's heart.

The next morning, Davey met Gus and Mister Thornton with mixed emotions. Silently, he handed back the book.

"I thought you might finish it," Gus commented. "So I brought another book by Mister London."

"*White Fang*," Davey read the title with a sense of gloom.

Responding to Davey's depression, Mister Thornton wormed his way onto the boy's lap. Davey stroked him gently as Gus began to read the story of the half-dog, half-wolf pup born in the Arctic wilderness. When he came to the part where the young animal was separated from, then reunited with, his mother, whose *"joy at finding him seemed greater even than his joy at being found,"* Davey stiffened.

"I hate my mother for leaving us," he stated with contempt. Gus studied him thoughtfully, but didn't respond.

It was early afternoon when they reached the end of the story which, to Davey's relief, concluded on a much happier note than *The Call of the Wild.*

"You now have two books from which to choose for your report," Gus stated gently.

"Maybe we could read together next week?" Davey asked hopefully.

"Of course. Until Monday, then," Gus responded.

The next day, Davey and his father visited friends at their camp in the Atchafalaya. It had been a long time since they had been to the swamp. Davey was thrilled when just the two of them were encouraged to take the little pirogue to bring in the traps, brimming with crawfish. As they glided through the still water, under a canopy of cypress trees dripping with Spanish moss, Davey's cares dissolved -- until that evening when his father danced too close with one of the guests. In a fit of rage, Davey rushed between them, pushing the woman away.

"What the devil's gotten into you?" his father demanded as he grabbed hold of Davey. But his anger soon turned to pity. "Davey," he told the boy softly, "your ma's not coming back. You've got to accept the fact that she's dead."

"No!" Davey screamed as he tore himself away.

When school came to a close on Monday, Davey met with Gus and Mister Thornton. At sight of his friend, Davey stopped in his tracks. The old man was dressed in a white linen suit, with a black bow tie and shoes. His snow-white hair appeared unkempt and his mustache seemed fuller, drooping beyond the corners of his mouth. Even his eyebrows were different. They were brushed up, their whiteness contrasting sharply against his wrinkled forehead.

"I ain't never seen a black Mark Twain," Davey remarked with a smile.

"Be that as it may," Gus replied good-naturedly, "at least you recognize the appearance of the best-known and loved of American writers."

Davey's smile faded. "Before she left, my ma read me *Tom Sawyer*," he stated softly.

"Then you have a background for the book I brought," Gus responded brightly.

"*The Adventures of Huckleberry Finn*," Davey read the title. "He was Tom's friend." Settling on the bench with Mister Thornton's head resting on his lap, Davey was soon transported into the story of another boy growing up along the Mississippi.

Later in the week, when they finished reading *Huckleberry Finn*, Gus brought *Captain Stormfield's Visit to Heaven*, also by Mark Twain. "It's about a riverboat captain who dreamed he went to heaven," Gus explained.

"I don't believe in heaven," Davey stated sullenly. "Or God," he added with contempt.

Gus studied him with kindness. "There is a saying that perplexes me. It is that God will not burden us with more than we can handle. But it is not God who causes bad things to happen. It was not God who caused your mother to go away."

"But the hurricane . . ," Davey bit back the rising tears.

"It wasn't God who built the levee," Gus offered softly. "There has been much talk on what God is all about," he continued. "The answer is quite simple. God is love. As much as we are hurt by life, God hurts even more for us. He does not exist to cause pain. He exists to help us through our pain."

Davey sat stiff and sullen, until Mister Thornton begged for his attention. As he stroked the little dog's head, the boy's anger melted into sadness.

On Friday, Miss Bouchard was pleased when Davey volunteered to give his book report. He chose to talk about *White Fang*. At the end of the day, he rushed to tell Gus of his success. But the old man and his little dog were nowhere to be found. It occurred to Davey that he could go to the high school to look for them.

"Can you tell me how I can find Mister Augustus Payne?" he asked the school secretary.

"There's no Mister Payne here," she responded as the janitor entered the office.

"He's a tutor," Davey explained. "He has a little dog named Buck Thornton."

The janitor looked up from his chores, his curiosity piqued by the boy's inquiry.

"I don't know any Mister Payne," the secretary responded before resuming her work.

Davey turned to go. The janitor followed him into the hallway. "Did you say you were lookin' for a Mister Payne?" he asked.

"Do you know him?" Davey asked hopefully.

"I once knew a Mister Augustus Payne. He was a teacher here when I was a boy. A sad, angry man. He taught English. He had a wife an' daughter who died in a tragic accident. Along with his little dog. But there's no way he could be the same Mister Payne you're lookin' for."

"Why not?"

"Because the Mister Payne I knew died many years ago."

Davey left the school in a daze. He wandered back to the bench where, to his astonishment, Gus waited with Mister Thornton.

"How . . . how is it . . . possible . . ?" the boy stammered.

"That we are here?" Gus asked gently. "It is possible through love," he explained. "Through your mother's love. She has not been able to find peace, knowing of your pain."

"Why couldn't she come?"

"Unfortunately, that's not how it works."

"I didn't even get to tell her good-bye," Davey responded with tears coursing down his cheeks.

"Ah, but that's the glory of it," Gus' eyes twinkled. "For you see, my child, there are no final good-byes."

Davey turned at the sound of a honking horn. From the car, his father motioned for Davey to join him. When Davey turned back, Gus and Mister Thornton had disappeared.

"Thank you, Gus . . . Thank you, Mister Thornton," Davey whispered. Smiling as he wiped away the tears, he went to join his father.

SHANE

The True Story of a Dog with a Heart of Gold

This was a first place winner for inspirational writing in a women's club competition.

Being a golden retriever, Shane was an accomplished swimmer. As such, he had absolutely no confidence in my swimming ability. He apparently thought I had no business being in a lake and felt it was his duty to "rescue" me by grabbing my arm and pulling me to shore. Repeatedly. When I would tire of his teeth marks, he would have me hang on to his tail. If I let go, he'd swim in a circle until I grabbed hold again. This from a dog who ordinarily didn't like anyone tugging on his tail.

When I relented to my younger son's pleas for a Chihuahua, I was concerned about Shane's acceptance of it. I needn't have worried. He treated little Samuelito el Bandito (Sami) with the same tenderness a mother elephant shows toward her young. He would regularly endure Sami's bouncing off his head, tugging at his ears, or playfully nipping his nose. When he had enough, with a gentle paw, Shane would simply push the little pest away.

Shane's gentleness was exhibited on numerous occasions. Such as when he adopted a tiny kitten that had apparently been abandoned. I was not in the market for a kitten. But, from the moment I saw them asleep together, with Tigger's little tawny body lost in Shane's magnificent golden coat, there was no way I could separate them.

The most endearing example of Shane's magnanimous nature was his nurturing of an orphaned fawn. Little Dove, named for the sign of God's love, was only a few days old when he was found, weak and shivering from shock, by the side of the road near my parents' cabin in Missouri. Through perseverance, we managed to convert him to a bottle. More than anything, it was Shane's devotion which replaced the love of Dove's absent mother. After grooming the wide-eyed infant, Shane would stand patiently and allow Dove to nuzzle him during the time of his, sadly, short-lived life.

When observing Shane's behavior toward the fawn, someone derisively commented on his being "a very confused dog." How sad. That the most pure form of Christ-like love and acceptance, one that transcended gender and species, would be viewed with any semblance of derision or suspicion.

At 13, Shane's sight grew dim and his body steadily deteriorated. But he was there when we called. And he came willingly, trustingly, on that sunlit day in August when the agonizing decision to relieve him of his increasing pain was carried out. Our vet agreed to make a house call and administered the coup-de-grace. Lying on the cool grass, with my sons and me stroking his silken body, bidding him a tearful farewell, we thanked Shane for his love and devotion as he calmly slipped away.

.

There is no doubt in my mind that animals go to heaven. If not, it wouldn't be Heaven. Shane's memory will live in our hearts forever, and will give us comfort until the time we again see his lopsided smile and shining coat. And we will never forget his example of pure love. If he had an epitaph, it would read:

Shane
His Heart Was Golden

This poem was inspired from a talk given by Ray Bradbury. I sent it to him, and he was kind enough to send me a copy of his book *Dinosaur Tales*, with the annotation: *"For Jeri Fonté, much thanks for your fine dinosaur poem! Love, Ray Bradbury."* It was a joy to have met him!

FOR THE LOVE OF DINOSAURS

Starry-eyed little boy
Led by the hand of his mother
Into worlds of wonder, reels of joy --
Cast upon a silver screen

In darkness came to life
All manner of imaginings
Pirates, kings, and every boys' delight --
Creatures from the dawn of time

The love of dinosaurs
Became this boy's longtime passion
That fueled his dreams and opened doors --
To live a life unequaled

Known and loved by millions
For works on stage, screen, and paper
The gratitude of generations --
For the love of dinosaurs

Jeri Fonté spent five months in East Africa with her two teenaged sons while researching her book *The Lure of the Lion.* During that time they camped for six weeks near Kenya's Maasai Reserve.

Josh Grossberg

Josh Grossberg is an award- winning journalist with more than 20 years of experience. His work has been published in far-flung publications, including the Los Angeles Times and the Kurdistan Times.

His articles have received local, state, and national recognition, including awards from the Associated Press, California Newspaper Publishers Association, Copley Newspapers and the Los Angeles Press Club.

Josh has published two anthologies of his work.

He currently works as Assistant City Editor at the Daily Breeze, a position he has held for six years. A lifelong Los Angeles resident, Josh currently resides in San Pedro

Tested but not Broken

It's been years since sunlight has touched her pale skin, but her husband will be by soon and she wants to look nice.

With delicate, fragile fingers, she reaches for her cosmetic case and, as an unwatched television flickers in the background, slowly daubs brush to makeup and then to her eyes, cheeks and lips. In a few minutes, her face shimmers with color and she smiles.

She's waiting for the sound of his footsteps down the hospital's long corridor.

It's a ritual Guadalupe Lara performs every morning in a life filled with rituals. There are the weekly visits with doctors, the daily visits from her husband, Amado, and the constant drone of a ventilator beside a bed she never leaves.

"This is my house," the 58-year-old says proudly. "My home."

For the past four years, home has been a corner room on the sixth floor, where Guadalupe is one of about 40 people in the care of a team of doctors, nurses and therapists. The patients live in the hospital's subacute ward, a place where people come when they've been injured in severe car accidents or violent crimes, sudden strokes or unlucky falls. Anybody at any time, in other words.

Many are in comas, others in a twilight world, half awake and half asleep, their only acknowledgment of the outside world is their fluttering eyelids. Some, such as Guadalupe, who suffers from lupus -- a chronic disease that causes the immune system to attack the body's own organs -- are too frail to be on their own.

The sixth-floor residents come from all backgrounds, but they mostly have a few things in common: the tracheotomies, ventilators that help them breathe and the tubes that nourish them.

And most of them will never leave. The average stay in this place is seven years. The longest, 17.

But, even in the face of death, this is a place where hope blooms, which is why Guadalupe has turned her small hospital room into a home. Around her are photographs -- hundreds of pictures of her son and her daughter, friends, siblings and parents. They're taped to walls and windows of her drab room, covering nearly every available space. There are pictures of her as a young girl in Mexico, pictures of birthdays and family gatherings. And there's a picture of her and Amado on their wedding day, a proud couple, young and untroubled, she in a white dress and looking like a young Natalie Wood, he in a suit and tie, his thin mustache perfectly trimmed.

"He is my angel," says Guadalupe with a broad smile, her face bloated by the medicine that keeps her alive.

They wed nearly 35 years ago. And now, with their anniversary approaching, Guadalupe has an idea: Why not do it again? If she's too frail to get to a church, why not renew her wedding vows in the hospital? And why not invite everybody she knows?

"I love this life," she says. "No matter how, I want it."

***

In the room next door, 39-year- old Carrie Reed sleeps quietly. Her boyfriend will be by soon, too. Like Amado Lara, Danny Smith comes every day to visit. He sits in Carrie's room for hours at a time, watching her still body and stroking her hair.

"She's very loving and caring," he says. "She cared about everybody."

One night a few years ago -- New Year's Eve 1999 -- Carrie said she felt ill. The couple had gone to a nearby Spires restaurant for dinner, but she had lost her appetite and didn't want to eat. After a few days, she wasn't any better and started to lose weight, so Danny took her to the doctor, who decided she was dehydrated and admitted her to the hospital. Danny isn't sure what happened next -- he suspects nurses gave her the wrong medicine -- but she slipped into a daze from which she never recovered.

"At 12 o'clock, she was fine," Danny says. "At 5 o'clock, she was slurring her words. She was wiped out. To this day I don't know what happened."

She teetered near death, but as her condition improved

slightly, Carrie was moved to the subacute ward, which would become her new home.

She couldn't talk, but Danny was convinced she could hear and understand him. In fact, by blinking her eyes, she was able to give him her power of attorney.

He came every day to visit. He'd show up in the morning on his way to work, during his lunch break and again at night after work.

"I finally got her to communicate," he says. "She smiled, moved her thumbs and started moving her head. I thought she was improving."

It was during one of these visits that Danny also had an idea. If he could get her to give him power over her affairs through the blinks of her eyes, maybe he could find a way to marry her.

"If it takes two or three years, I'll be here no matter what," he says.

***

Each day the sixth floor begins like the one before it: An aide enters the patients' room and pins a piece of paper printed with the day of the week to the wall. While many won't notice it, for others it's the only tangible reminder of the comings and goings of days and months and years.

For those on the other end -- the hospital workers and caregivers -- life in the subacute ward can be unlike anywhere else in the hospital. Day after day, they get to know their patients. They share holidays and birthdays with them. They celebrate their victories, fret when they become ill and mourn when they die.

"There's always hope," says Alvin Munoz, a registered nurse who runs the ward. "If the sun shines and there's air to breathe, we try to make it a better day."

Doctors visit weekly, and there are regular meetings of nurses, respiratory therapists, dietitians, pharmacists, activities coordinators and family members to ensure the patients are well taken care of.

It's a strange place for familial bonds to form, but they can be deep and lasting. When Guadalupe has a rough day, the staff hovers like worried parents. And Danny has become so fond of the staff that he brings them presents.

"They take care of me as much as they take care of Carrie," he says. "They're like angels."

The feeling is mutual. In a place where recovery is rare, the friendly face can be a cherished commodity.

"He hates hospitals, but his devotion inspires us," Alvin says. "But since the patient is going to live here, we try to make the best of it."

In fact, despite the often grim circumstances, it's hard to find a face that isn't smiling; as doctors, nurses and aides walk up and down the corridors, they offer a friendly hello to visitors.

Everybody notices Maria Retana's smile. Being an activities assistant for people who, at best, can hardly move, might seem like an odd choice for a career, but for Maria and the ward's two other coordinators, it's a calling.

Twice a day, a small group of patients is wheeled into a large room for their activity period. For some, it might mean eking a little movement out of their muscles by playing with blocks. For those who can't even do that, the day's activity might include having a little jar of coffee or nutmeg waved under their nose.

"We do sensory stimulation," Maria says. "We try to get a response with things they're familiar with."

Patients may seem totally unaware of their surroundings, but a whiff of a scent they're acquainted with can cause their nose to twitch, or even a smile to cross their face.

And when that happens, Maria beams and giggles.

"It took me four or five months to say I can handle this job," she says. "But I don't think I could do anything else."

It would be easy to forget about these people, to leave them in their rooms and pretend they're not there. But for Maria, that's simply not an option.

"When they pass away, a little piece of me goes with them," says the 31-year-old.

After working in a nursing home, Maria switched careers to work at a school. But she missed the contact with patients.

"I like to help people who are in need," she says. "Somehow I need them, too. Three quarters of these people have nobody or they have people who don't care."

***

As holidays approach, the walls and ceilings of the sixth floor become festooned with decorations: Santas at Christmas, ghouls at Halloween.

"We try to keep things like they used to be," Alvin says.

But things aren't like they used to be, and for most, never will be.

Not for people such as Kalice Knox. A handsome 24-year-old, Kalice can open his eyes and stare, giving the impression that he's awake. Or he can smile when he hears his mother's voice, but the small bump on his head shows why he's probably going to spend the rest of his life in a hospital. While attending a party in 1997, a bullet pierced his brain. He was at a friend's house, and when his mother came to pick him up, he was sitting in a chair next to a window with a hole in it. It was the day before his birthday.

His mother, Mae Knight, enjoys their time together. She lovingly strokes his arm, and he knows that she's there. And she's philosophical about his condition.

"We communicate with our eyes," she says. "He was pretty wild, in and out of trouble. I guess this slowed him down. That's the way I see it. He slowed down, but he's still here."

Not everybody has visitors. One man who has been in the ward for six months not only spends his days shut off from the world by a coma, he doesn't even have a name. Known by the staff only as John Doe, his life and history remain a mystery.

And 57-year-old Dorothy Carr, who is trapped inside a broken body but has a clear mind. She watches the world from her wheelchair after suffering from a stroke, hungers for a decent meal she'll never be able to eat and, if the weather is nice, is taken outside once a week for a little fresh air.

With her one good hand, she can scrawl one-word messages. When asked what she misses most about being a prisoner in her own body, she scribbles: "Food. Water. Can't talk."

But she's still alive, which means the staff treats her with dignity. During an activity session, Maria holds up bottles of nail polish and asks her what color she likes. Dorothy responds with a slight nod and watches as Maria carefully applies paint to her fingers. It's a job few will notice, but Maria treats it seriously. As a few drops of polish run to the skin around the nail, she meticulously wipes it away with cotton. Respectfully calling her "Mrs. Carr," Maria also takes the opportunity to tease and even manages to coax a half-smile out of her.

"She feels so helpless," Maria says. "I pray with her, and we read the Bible together. It comforts her."

***

Amado Lara is 21 years older than his wife, so he never imagined he'd be the one who would be taking care of her. But he looks far younger than his 79 years and doesn't mind the long drive every morning to visit her.

He came to California from Mexico, took a job as a laborer and then worked for a railroad. One night in 1966, a friend urged him to check out the scene at a dance hall in East Los Angeles. It cost $5 to get into the Flamingo, so Amado was reluctant, but his friend convinced him.

"When I met him, I knew right away," says Guadalupe, who was there that night. "His character, everything about him. I felt butterflies in my stomach. I knew he's my love forever."

"I played guitar a lot and she loved it," Amado says. "She was educated and loved dancing and communicating."

The lupus started taking its toll in 1982. At first it was more of an annoyance and she braved the pain.

"I continued with my life," she says. "We went to Mexico every year, went to Canada."

She loved to cook and feed her family and friends, but about 20 years ago, the disease worsened and so did the pain. She spent time in various hospitals and went back home for a while. Amado tried his best to look after her, even sleeping on the floor next to her bed, but after a few days, it became too difficult.

"I kept her at home for 13 days, but she felt I had no chance to go shopping for groceries," he says. "I had to give her medicine, clean her suction hose."

By now, her bones have become so fragile that she broke both of her legs last year when she tried to stand up.

So, Amado arrives daily for his visits, where he sits next to her bed, holds her hand and talks with her about their lives and two children. The only time they disagree is when they turn on the television.

"I love sports, but she loves the novellas (Spanish soap operas)," he says. "Before I didn't like them, but I'm getting used to them."

Guadalupe also spends her days planning for her Oct. 1 anniversary. The family has been invited, a priest hired. In the months leading up to the day, Guadalupe sits in her bed, surrounded by bags of beads and lace, making intricate baskets she will give to each of her guests. She attached each ribbon, each paper flower by hand, slowly making sure it's all perfect.

It may not have been the way he planned to spend his retirement years, but Amado can't think of anything he'd rather be doing. As for the future, they're both realistic.

"We all have to die," Amado says. "We are mortal, and we all have to die."

"God gave me today," Guadalupe says. "If God gives me tomorrow, that's wonderful."

As evening approaches, Amado returns home, but his day isn't finished. The couple's daughter suffered a childhood accident and is now brain damaged. Although she has a job, she can't read and Amado needs to make dinner for her. In fact, he makes the trip back and forth to the hospital twice a day.

"If something happens to me, my daughter is lost," he says.

***

The first time Danny saw Carrie at a Little League game, he knew she was something special.

"I looked at her and thought, `Man, what a beautiful woman,' " he says.

Too shy to speak, he kept his peace until one day he found

himself standing next to her in line at the snack bar.

"I was so scared," he says. "I was standing beside her and I gave her a kiss and said, `I love you.' It was either do or die. It was true, solid love ever since."

The year was 1995. Danny was in his early 40s, Carrie Reed in her early 30s when they decided to move in together. Even though they both had children, they went ahead.

"With kids it was kind of rough, but we struggled through it," he says.

Danny remembers times and places as if they were markers along a road. They were watching Dick Clark's New Year's Eve show when Carrie became ill. He took her to the doctor on Jan. 16. On Jan. 19, they watched "Little House on the Prairie" together. At noon, on the 20th, she seemed to be OK, but five hours later, he noticed she was slurring her words and then she started to throw up.

"I'll regret this for the rest of my life, but I went home," Danny says. "I called the next morning, and they said she was sent to the ICU. I called later, and they told me there was no way she was going to make it through the night. To this day, I don't know what happened."

Carrie made it through the night, but she never regained consciousness. By the time she moved to the subacute ward, she weighed 69 pounds -- a skeleton with skin draped over it is how Danny describes it.

***

The first few years were hard for Guadalupe. But now, even when she's having a rough day, she's invariably in a good mood. She acts coy when asked why she's so happy, saying a little birdie told her a secret, but with a little coaxing, begins to tell a story. It's hard for her to talk, but in halting sentences, punctuated by deep, rasping breaths, she begins:

"The first year was a bad year. I wanted to die. I'm angry with God, with people, my family, even my husband and my daughter. I don't want to see nobody. I made a letter to disconnect the machine and I gave it to my son. I didn't want to fight anymore. I was tired. People were walking and laughing and I couldn't.

"My son told me, `Mom is that what you want? If you want this, I'll do it for you. I love you so much, but if you want to do that, I'll do it for you. But it's not you, it's your anger.'

"I saw the expression on his face. It was like a knife in my heart and I couldn't do it. I started to cry and cry.

"And I said, `I'm sorry, I love you so much, I can't do that. I can't go. If it's painful, it's OK.'

"That night, I felt something blow in my ear, but there was nobody here. I didn't feel scared. It was our Father. I said, `I'm in pain, pain all night, I can't move my legs. It's terrible, but God, I'm in your hands.' And he told me, `My daughter, you're OK.' The room smelled like a lily. The next day, I moved my legs and my hands. At first nobody believed me, but there's no pain anymore."

***

It's one thing to work with adult patients in this situation, but Alvin can't bring himself to work with comatose children.

In fact, there are no children in the subacute ward. There are special facilities for children -- as young as infants -- who might fall into a swimming pool and need to spend their entire lives under professional care.

"I can't handle being with children," he says. "I have two kids of my own. Hospitals can't even get staffs for them."

Every now and again, almost miraculously, a patient will wake up and leave the ward. While it can be a blessed event for that patient's family, it can also fill the ward with the false hope that maybe it will happen again. That's when Alvin is forced to once again help families come to the understanding that their loved ones are never going to get better.

"Some people are in denial," he says. "Some hospitals don't prepare family members what to expect. Sometimes when they come here, they don't know how bad the condition is."

***

Carrie is gaining weight, and Danny is feeling encouraged. He's hoping she'll recover soon, and he's still planning to get married.

He kept up his visits, and even when she needed an

operation to install a new feeding tube, Danny remained optimistic, telling a visitor to come back in a few days so he can meet her.

But she developed an infection and ended up needing five surgeries in 10 days. But er fragile couldn't handle and Carrie finally died. She was 39.

"They let me lay beside her for four days straight," Danny says. "I was with her all the way till the end, stayed talking to her for hours."

***

After months of preparation and anticipation, it's time. Guadalupe and Amado are going to renew their wedding vows. It's a Saturday morning, but it seems the entire hospital staff arrives in formal attire. Relatives come from all over the county and Mexico. They arrive at the hospital, are given identification stickers and then ushered into a conference room.

Meanwhile, in Guadalupe's room, Maria shows up early to help the bride prepare. Guadalupe wears a white wedding dress specially crafted so she can put her arms through the sleeves without having to get out of bed.

Amado nervously paces in a suit and tie. He's been banished from the room because it would be bad luck for him to see his bride.

As the guests assemble, Amado takes his place next to the priest. Alvin is his best man and stands beside him.

Danny is here, too, and sits quietly, keeping mostly to himself in the back of the room.

"It's a shame I couldn't pull off what's happening here," he says. "Maybe someday I'll understand, maybe I won't. But it's impossible to put into words the love I feel for these people and this place."

Finally, Guadalupe, accompanied by three nurses, is wheeled into the room. Children run up to her and they hug. Guadalupe glows with joy.

While her ventilator whines behind the couple, a priest begins the ritual. He goes through the traditional recitations in both Spanish and English as Guadalupe and Amado hold hands and softly repeat their lines.

"In sickness and in health?" the priest says.
"In sickness and in health," they repeat.
"Until death do you part?"
"Until death do us part."

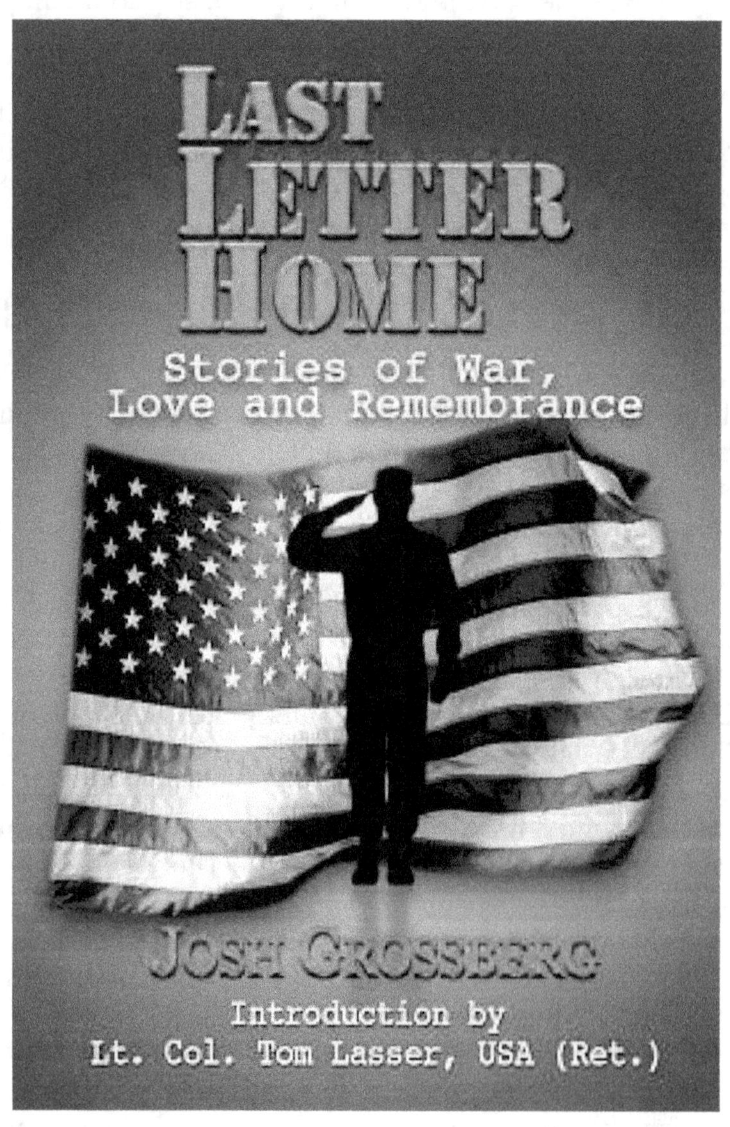

Judy Sunderland

Judy Sunderland is a freelance writer living in Torrance, CA. She previously wrote for *The Poughkeepsie* Journal and was Editor-in-Chief of *The Dutchess Chronicle.* Judy holds a BA in Creative Writing from the State University of New York, New Paltz, a certificate in Creative Writing from UCLA Extension program and an MFA from Antioch University, Los Angeles. She has no idea what she wants to do when she "grows up." Judy has a very eclectic employment history and considers any job to be fodder for her writing career. Past positions include working as a receptionist for a mental hospital, preparing personal income taxes, tutoring English at a community college, routing ambulances and tow trucks, grooming horses and maintaining technical manuals for the United States Army, Navy and Air Force. She is proudly married to a rocket scientist and the love of her life, Dr. Dave, an internationally known Karaoke stylist.

DOUBLE ON, DOUBLE OFF

We step into the Stockyard carefully, so our eyes can adjust to the dark. It is always noisy and crowded on Friday and until one can see, it is best to be cautious. Suki, our favorite pub hostess, waves us over to our customary corner barstools. She motions to Don, the bartender, and slides a dainty handful of red, enameled claws across Jimmy's shoulders. As Don sets our usual orders on napkins in front of us she purrs, "Deese on me, for my bes customers. You ear'y today, you want to order lunsch now?" Her accent is easier to understand after an hour or two of drinking.

"Thank you, Suki. I'll have the Sourdough." I hang my bag on the hook under the bar (I surely didn't want to put it on the floor in that sawdust) and straddle my stool. I verbally hand Suki off to Jimmy's wife, Marion, "You gonna eat?"

"Yeah, Chef salad? Put the blue cheese on the side. And Jimmy will have the same." Marion looks at her husband and smiles fondly. "All those pretzels tonight, babe. You should watch it today."

Jimmy smiles playfully and pickes up Suki's hand by a dragon-lady nail and rubs it between his thumb and index finger. "O.K" he says, "And maybe I shouldn't have blue cheese or onions on the salad."

"How about oil and vig-nig-ger? Enjoy you lunsch." Suki pulls her hand back reluctantly and slides over to greet the next patrons.

I purse my lips and looked at Marion. It's a common tease we share, I say, "You know he only orders like that to hear Suki stumble over the words. He's cruel."

Jimmy smiles in over-feigned innocence, "I've got those Japanese investors coming in this afternoon. I don't want my breath to offend."

I glance around the room. In better days, this place had been a classy piano bar. Now it is the local lunch hang out for the Wilshire Boulevard business crowd. We all come here for the food, strong drinks, and to hide office romances in the dimly lit, red vinyl booths.

"Why didn't you treat them to lunch with us? What better way to impress clients than to show them the American businessman's lunch scene? Can you imagine how everybody would run when they saw all your clients, with all their cameras?"

We all laugh.

Marion changes the subject and looks at me closely. "Are you ready for tonight?"

I smile as casually as I can and I lie. "Really, I haven't thought much about it. I didn't want to get nervous. I don't even know who I'm supposed to beat tonight."

Marion looks disbelieving. She offers, "I went by the pub last night and looked at the board." Marion counts off on her fingers. "Shawn Trent, from Mucky Duck, lost to our Sherry last night at Kingshead Pub, so you need to beat Des himself from Des Regan's."

"Oh, my God. Not himself." My pulse zips a little quickstep and I say, "I haven't beaten him yet."

"No, but I bet you'd like to." Jimmy makes an obscene gesture under the bar.

I turn my hot face away and sip my water. "Shut up and eat your lunsch."

It's a long afternoon and I have a rough time keeping my mind on my computer screen. I guess being a surety bond underwriter for an uptown insurance broker has its exciting moments, but I'd be hard-pressed to name one, even under the best of circumstances. I drive home without the usual hand gestures and curse words. I put the car on autopilot and consider my strategy for the evening match. I really need a plan.

Frustrated beyond belief, standing in the center of my room clad in a black unitard, I feel like some blubbery, inadequate, new age seal. I scan myself critically while turning in front of the mirror. I'm not slender enough to be fashionable, but I don't regret that. Men like to dance with me and hold me close. Discarded clothing hangs from my chair, desk and bedposts like silky Spanish moss. What am I going to wear over this? Think, I tell myself. Concentrate. Any of my colorful gypsy skirts would be appropriate. Except...the wide waistband of the blue, green, and yellow parrot skirt always makes my hips look enormous. If I add a big shirt for contrast, I draw attention away from my cleavage. Think. I bend forward and pick up my favorite, solid green crinkle skirt for the fourth time. There is a small, but irritating bleached spot right in the lap. It will be dark in the pub, and it will really show. No distractions for me tonight, please God. I have to win. I decide to wear the unitard without a skirt. I hang a jangly (distracting) belt of gold coins around my hips and slip my arms into an extra-long, Kelly green jacket with gold Celtic dogs embroidered on the lapels. I add my favorite piece of jewelry; my mother's large, gold chain and Celtic cross which hangs down between my breasts in just the right spot. I lace my feet into an old pair of gillies. There, that's the look. Casual, with just a hint of tradition. Inspired by the gillies, I skip a few steps towards the bathroom. I turn up the volume and hum along with the bouncy reel playing on my IPod.

I pull my hair back and anchor it with a black velvet band and consider, again, cutting my bangs. No, I like my forehead clean. Des once commented on my long, thick, and as he put it, "enticing" hair. The unusual golden-auburn streak that runs through it is a family trait. I can thank my sainted mother (may she rest in peace and dance w' the angels) for it. The next tune, a traditional waltz, floods the room. "Her eyes, they shone like diamonds, you'd think she was queen of the land." I croon along. With my Pearson's bristle brush, I stroke my hair until it crackles with electricity. I lean in to the mirror, spread neutral-toned eye shadow, and apply my mascara lightly. It won't do to look too made up tonight. Sexy, but clean, alluring and fresh-faced, that's the look I know he likes. As I do my hair I watch the steam rising from the tight coils of red-gold wrapped around the curling iron. I strategically dab White

Shoulders on my wrists and behind my ears and into my cleavage.

I pack my bag. Which sets to take? All of my darts are professional. My favorite titanium shaft, 18 oz., "torpedoes," of course. I grab two other sets, one medium and one lightweight. I check to be sure that my favorite zodiac and Harp beer flights are in the pocket, along with several other sets. I feel around for my chalk, record book and note my financial status. sixty bucks, cash. Enough. It wouldn't do to be poorly prepared. The guys are counting on me. Luck is with me tonight; I can taste it.

I walk into Molly's and find my team, the Loose Cannons, waiting for me. These guys are the best. Although I regularly earn my way into the playoffs, there is some serious side-betting going on for this one. My teammates kinda tricked me into this, with their boasting and of course, they are here to cheer me on. Although Molly's is not my home court, I play here frequently enough to be confident. As I sit down, a pint of Bass magically appears on the bar in front of me.

"Slainte," Jimmy says, and we tip our pints.

The cool ale goes down quickly and I notice that Jimmy seems a little loaded already. "Where's Marion?"

"Home. She may show up later, but I think she only said that to keep me in line." He shrugged and his eyes twinkled at me. "You know how it is."

I nod and smile. In fact, I do know how it is. Jimmy's philandering is legendary and he and I have had our share of adventure together. I hope Marion shows up though. I hate having to take Jimmy home when he's drunk. Our past is past and he does not seem to remember that when he's been drinking.

I consult the board. The match should start eight and it is now a quarter of. "So, where's my competition? You think he's gonna chicken out on me?" I say, and I raise my glass, drain it and dab the damp bar napkin innocently on my chest. The air-conditioning doesn't work well in this old building.

"Lord, woman, you look like you're trolling for a little rooty-tooty tonight. I hope you're concentrating on the board, and not the boy, and," Jimmy says, with a nod, "he's standing right behind you."

I hope he didn't hear that. I turn on my stool to confront Des. His cornflower blue eyes have a deceptively sleepy look to them. His tiny smile tells me he heard. How long was he watching me?

"Des," I nod and hold out my hand. "Good luck tonight."

"Judy," Des says, "Same to you. I might say, let the best man win, but for obvious reasons, I won't."

That accent of his melts me. My hand is firm, if a little moist, as we shake. I hold his hand a tiny bit longer than necessary, then drop it slowly, trailing my fingers across his palm. I breathe deeply and see his eyes move downward, to watch my cross rise and fall. All the better to beat you with, my dear.

The bartender rings the bell and all eyes turn to Jimmy.

"It was agreed previously, one game each, five-oh-one, double on, double off. The winner will be allowed to call himself, or herself, the best dart player in the valley without dispute." Jimmy smiles at us and holds up a coin. "Desmond Regan, are you ready? Judy O'Kelley, are you ready?" We nod. Des wins the toss.

He stands at the line and grips his dart lightly in gentle, manicured fingers. The spotlights pointed at the board create deep shadows on the faces of the gallery. I notice how his chest hairs curl around his half-buttoned shirt and nearly bury the gold Saint Christopher that hangs around his neck. I watch the ripples of muscle in his arms through his soft, gray cotton shirt. Des makes one, two aiming feints and tosses his dart with a lightning thrust. It's buried almost to the hilt in the bristle-board. Twenty. He misses the double twenty twice more. He's not on.

I move to center stage. I hold my darts casually as I breathe deeply. I focus on the double ring while I bring my first dart up. One, two, it flies, swift and sure to the double twenty. I don't hear the cheers of my mates. I have two more throws. Like metallic dragonflies, my remaining two darts zip to the board. Fifteen and double fifteen, looking good. Now I can smile. I step up and twist out my darts; I toss my hair back over my shoulders, making sure to stand where the light will pick out my highlights.

Des smiles and takes a moment for a sip of his Guinness. Over the rim of his pint, he watches me move to my stool. He wipes the foam from his upper lip, steps up to the line and with an unmanly grace throws three darts in rapid succession. Double twenty, double twenty, double twenty. The gallery sucks in a collective, appreciative breath before it cheers.

"Nice darts." I say. I stand and, lacing my fingers together, stretch my arms out over my head and then pull them behind me and push out my chest. I breathe deeply again and take up my darts.

With an evil precision, I toss a double twenty, ten, and double ten. I watch the scorekeeper tally my numbers with his chalk. Three-forty-six. Not great, but not bad. Jimmy has pulled my darts and he motions me to the table at the side, just out of the light. From the sidelines, I scan Des' face. If he's stressing, it doesn't really show. The muscles of his arms are tense, but he holds the darts gently. His fingertips caress the sharp edges of the peach colored flights that I know are his favorites. I can almost feel the ridges on the grips of the titanium shafts in his delicate fingertips. Snap, sssnap, sssnap. His missiles tear holes in the delicate smoke curtain before embedding themselves in the bristles of the board. He chalks up a formidable lead; two more double twenties and a double nineteen. As he passes me, he smiles, shows me his perfect teeth and reaches out to pat my arm. I ignore him and take up my darts. Carefully I aim. I concentrate on the center of the board. My entire world has shrunk down to this incredibly tiny, dark, circle in the exact center of the universe. As the shaft leaves my fingers, I know it is wrong. The arc is crooked, I score another twenty. I adjust my stance and glance over at Des. He is sitting on a high stool with his arms folded across his chest. He has rolled his sleeves up and the incredibly blond hair on his forearms practically glows in the dark.

He knows I am looking at him. He nods almost imperceptibly. I toss my head to clear it and wiggle my fingers.

I toss my other darts. Oh, almost. A fifty and a triple twenty. I pull my darts and brush past Des to get a refill. I sit on his stool.

He stands in the light with his strong legs slightly apart. As he glances over to where I am sitting, I bite my lower lip and pull it through my teeth slowly while I breathe deeply. He smiles and tosses his darts off casually. Trip twenty, trip fifteen, trip ten.

"Oh, Jeez," says Jimmy, "he's found the triple ring. Get up there, girl, and take him."

Wouldn't I like to? I assume my stance. I have to make up over one hundred points just to catch up. I glance at him. Des salutes me with his pint and smiles confidently. His eyes twinkle in the reflected light and I wonder what he would be like in... I toss my hair over my shoulder, raise my darts and toss the first two with rapid-fire accuracy. A dead center bull's eye, and a double sixteen. Thank you, God. The crowd sighs. They know the remaining thirty-four is my lucky double shot.

"Nice darts. Before I shoot my last, shake my hand," says Des, and extends his big hands. "After all, we're still good friends and this is just a game."

His palm is damp from the sweat of his beer mug, but it is a warm, moist wet. His other hand pats the back of my wrist. His eyes are a little distant. My triumph of a few moments ago is over. There is no hesitation in his throws. One, two, three, his scores are exact and final. A double nineteen, trip twenty and a double fifteen. The gallery screams and hoots. Animal sounds reverberate from the walls and off the wooden floor. Des glows in the spotlight and is slapped repeatedly on the back while his arm is wrung nearly out of its socket.

I smile bravely at my teammates and shrug my shoulders. They look nearly as crushed as I feel. I force my way into Des' crowd to offer my congratulations. "Excellent game," I say, "You are the best player in the valley." I bow to him. "Can I buy you a beer?"

"Surely, that'd be lovely. You know, you play well, for a girl." Des smiles mischievously as we work our way through the crowd to claim a corner booth.

I answer his smile and watch his eyes as I slip off my jacket. "You beat me fair and square," I say generously. I lean forward, resting my breasts on my folded arms. “What'll you have?"

***

Laura Hines-Jurgens

Laura Hines Jurgens graduated Magna Cum Laude from CSULB. She was awarded the Sylvia Russell Award for Equality and Justice in Ecology and the Sharyn DiSanza Award for Equality and Justice through Artistic Expression. These honors are from Feast, Inc., a Women Without Borders environmental group. An exhibiting artist for fifteen years, she also serves the arts community as curator and juror-most recently for the national, GLOBAL WARMING: Artists Speak Exhibition, for the Orange County Center for Contemporary Arts. She and her work are featured in two DVDs: ***Global Warming-Healing Hands,*** and ***Stop Global Warming,*** directed by Steve Gooden of No Compromise Films. The films are documentary shorts derived from the artists' process and paintings in her eco-struggle. Locally, her work is showcased in the book, ***The Palos Verdes Peninsula Artists,*** by Stephen Smoke, and ***Palos Verdes Style Magazine*** Editor, Lili Miura, MS Publishing. Regionally, she gives artist talks with slides and Keynote presentations on global warming using her paintings and eco-art pieces from exhibitions she has curated. As an environmental speaker for adults and children, her global warming subjects include habitat stress, environmental destruction and the strain wars and overpopulation place on the planet. Hines-Jurgens' work has been exhibited in solo and group shows regionally, nationally and internationally (Giorgio de Chirico Museum, Greece). E-mail: ***LHJFineArts@aol.com.***

DATING HQ:
SHAPING MARRIAGE *BEFORE* IT BEGINS

First Date

I found it is not a good idea to judge the first draft of anything: art, music, ideas, especially dating. Everyone I ever asked said dating was really fun. So, when the doorbell rang I was ready to have fun.

I'd known him since the sixth grade. We hadn't talked much before he asked me out to the school outing, and I can't remember much of the date. It was awkward. No, it was worst than awkward. It was gawky, tense and embarrassing. I didn't know what to say! I kept wondering when the fun would start. Then I started wondering *if* the fun would start. Finally, I wondered why I agreed to a date at all. I looked at the older girls, they seemed like they were doing better at this than I was. Maybe it was me. The afternoon passed like a big bunch of nothing.

I took it out on my journal. After three pages of ink describing fun as boring, I decided to check out how the dictionary described it.

Fun / n. & adj. There were several definitions. I focused on *"lively or playful,"* and *"exciting or amusing goings-on".* Well, that explains it! We didn't do anything! I can't imagine a bump on a log has much fun either.

My Mom asked me how my date went. When I told her, she suggested, "Maybe you should tell your friends some of your stories. I like them."

I thought about what my Mom said about my stories. I sulked over her confidence in me, but finally decided I'd work on it. I like fun stories, so I went for the comic approach.

I figured out a date was not just something to show up for. It can be that, but for the date to be memorable, I had to be a big part of it. Participation was key! So was timing. I'd wait until the conversation was at a low point and I'd talk it back up with some incident from school, the latest gossip, jokes, bloopers or a funny news point and like magic, the party was back in play.

I found out that anyone who can carry off a good story can change things, like feelings, a mood or an attitude! My stories picked up the ho-hums, and while I had his attention I'd question him about something I wanted to know.

Laughter pries loose ideas. Happy people peel off their chips, get relaxed and even add other stories. When ideas bounce around a group, it creates more of everything except boredom. The results of my stories produced fun second dates, third, etc., and caused my weekends to be spent with colorful types who played with their imagination, had many opinions and thought my ideas were imaginative.

Problem Solving

My early creative start came due to the lack of funds. I considered myself a fix-it type. I'd flash on an idea, think it out and put it together. If it didn't work, I'd redo it until it did or let it morph into something I liked even better. I now recognize what I was doing is called problem solving. In high school, it started, I had continuous, rotating activities. This story is one of my projects.

Marriage had a bad reputation in my mind. In High School I saw it start with the flirty, beauty queens. Guys hovering around them and their friends. They'd get married shortly after they graduated, get pregnant, get fat, get pregnant again and then the stories of their fights would start circulating around. Before long the husbands were out with other women, and after a while these guys didn't even seem to care that their secrets were out or that their wives knew about the infidelity. Next up, divorce and the beauty queen was back living with Mom, working as a waitress at the local diner so she could buy shoes for her kids.

That story was repeated so many times, I figured it was probably best I not participate. Besides early marriage did not fit with my plans. The big M and kids, not for me! I liked unique. On a date, I wanted to have fun, and get into a guy's mind and find out what he thought; his goals and plans.

Great for him but I am writing this story because I can't remember having any ambitions past being a standup comic. At that point, it would have been great to have had a story like this. So, I guess it is true, we write the material we want to read.

After high school and a year into working dumb jobs, I packed up my stories and carried myself back to school. In college I found many opportunities to learn to think . . . about the world and really amazing things in the world . . . and about myself, my future ambitions and goals . . . and for out-of-town dates. Dating at other universities was another opportunity to try out my material on new guys. Everyone likes to laugh.

My favorite subjects were English and Art. I advanced to developing my stories on the page, talking about them on dates and painting them out on canvas. Great, huge canvases.

Happily, I finished college but I wanted to have time to continue my storytelling and artwork. To pay the rent, I picked up more boring jobs. My process now included writing artist statements to accompany the artwork. Painting story messages in color, using brushes, scrapers, sticks and rags on large, odd-shaped canvases is the love of my life. My paintings are loosely based on experiences I've had with people I've known. I mix up allegories, incidental humor, drama and tragedy.

The paintings are like my dating stories, not preachy but with a point.

Divorce Rates

Change rolled in when I started to notice the divorce rates rise among my friends. Even the couples that stayed together didn't seem happy in their marriages. I concluded that people were getting married, just to get married. Like it was part of a check-off list of things to do. I was puzzled, that didn't seemed like the right reason to get married. Then somebody told me starting in the 1970's, half the marriages ended in divorce.

If marriage was failing the very people who believe in it, something must be wrong with the model. It is a strange problem. I resolved to check it out. It seemed impossible that their last happy day be the one when they say, 'I do.' There are so many ominous statistics about the divorce rates that even while throwing the bouquet a distant rumble of anxiety is felt. The new dishes are hardly out of the box when couples are not having discussions; they are fighting about incidentals.

Refresh and Renew

Any set of standards failing most of its clients, probably needs to be modified, altered or changed, if it is going to continue. Divorce was creating insecure, anxious people who had been hoping for the 'happily ever after' dream, married couples want.

I needed solution information. Something new, to reshape the culture of marriage before it begins. I wanted a plan, a pathfinder to guide people through and out of this topsy-turvy alphabet of complication and risks. I went looking for a reliable format, a language, something user-friendly and personal, to get a head start on marital success.

What I discovered was an obsolete dating philosophy, circa: the rule of the grandfathers. It is time to change the formula, throw out the old playbook and update the rules. The road this aging system travels on needs an upgrade. Marriage has ceased to be the central organizing principle in peoples' lives because it has become so prone to failure.

To paraphrase a report in the ***New York Times,*** *No Easy Fix**, Nick Schulz comments on the collapse of intact households. "The gap has widened to include all sorts of disparities, especially income. Social resources play a huge role in helping couples get ahead. With the institution of marriage, the primary route for inculcating human and societal capital, the potential for those not in a stable home environment to find economic success is also compromised. The problem of marital breakdown doesn't lend itself to easy fixes."

**LAT. Op-ed, p. A-27, No easy fix. By Nick Schulz (references 99ers)*

My reasoning took 'normal' out of marriage. There is no 'normal' anymore, and 'typical' is past tense. Time to reset the pace to 'refresh and renew.' Couples go into marriage for more than the chemistry, they are ready to settle down and expect some predictability. This means there is a need to reduce the issues that create the uncertainty. Couples want a more effective family foundation, away from lurking divorce fears.

What was needed was a change in the framework. Talking with divorced friends, it seemed the common denominator was they got married too soon. While they were dating they didn't talk much and were married before they knew much about each other. Of course they were in love, but had never given themselves the chance or the time to learn to like each other.

The same wishes and desires kept coming up. Divorced women wanted individualized loose, personal structures to grow decision-making powers. Now they wanted to learn about themselves before it came time to choose a marriage partner. That information took me back to the basics: dating, talking, getting to know each other. Seems straightforward enough, so how to accomplish it.

The List

'My friends' does not constitute a huge study group, but so many of the same themes kept rubbing up against the same problems, I felt the solution was texting itself to me when a thought bubble rippled up one morning with Cinderella in it. There she was in the form of an idea. 'Make up a list of ones hopes and dreams.'

I thought about it. Having a Hopes and Dreams list could act like a GPS system. It could point a woman in the direction she wants to go. When she knows where she wants to go, she can talk about it, and plan how to get there. Hopes and dreams need not adhere to any standards. Just get started writing. Ask for glass slippers if that gets pen moving on the pad in your hand.

Having a list to work from, makes it easier to ask people

to give you their opinions on the various listed ambitions. Everybody has opinions. Asking questions about your special ideas and getting answers, gives a woman perspective.

The list is not set in stone. It can grow or change. Additions and subtraction wiggle themselves in and out and that's O.K. too.

From this list, grow hard questions (HQ) to ask dates. I call them hard questions, not because they are hard for him, he only has to give an answer. The HQ are hard for you, because you have to think them up. His answers provide clarity and understanding. A chance for a woman to get to know him. He has no reason to lie, and if he does she will eventually find out.

Future, potential dates are decided, based on his reactions and answers to your questions. He either likes the way you think or not. Dream seekers need champions. Ambitions need encouragement and support. At the end of the day a woman wants to meet her goal at the finish line, not divorce papers.

So the objective becomes a personal design. A woman creates *a loose framework* to grow the decision-making powers she needs to understand and implement her goals. This knowledge then starts to change the statistics about why marriage becomes unhappy and fails.

There are some things that seem deep and mystifying. For instance: who would be a good husband and who would be a bad husband, and how to choose. The sister to Reese Witherspoon's character, in the movie, *This Means War,* told her, "don't choose the best guy, choose the guy that's going to make you the best girl."

This may seem complicated. Below is a how-to guide. In summary, it makes divorce the villain, and marital success the easy goal.

How to Tell a Bad Guy?

No one wears a sign that says, "Stay away! I'm a bad guy!" The following, however, is a way for you decide.

It has nothing to do with him looking like a criminal. It has nothing to do with him being the guy your friends told you to stay away from. It has nothing to do with his job or what he looks like, his extracurricular activities, who likes him or not . . . Its all about his answers to your questions. He could be tall, dark and handsome with great body language and a fantastic smile but, you will know he is not going to be a good guy *for you,* when he opens his mouth and the words that come tumbling out in response to your HQ turn all your dials to *off*! That is how you can tell who is a bad guy. Good chance he won't even like you asking him your hard questions.

How to Identify a Good Guy?

Your list and your questions are a huge part of the safety factor in determining who you can relax and possibly fall in love with. The "good guy" is not wearing a halo and dressed in white. You know what I'm suggesting here . . . He is the guy who answers your hopes and dreams questions to your satisfaction.

That kind of evaluation drives you and your dreams in the right direction. Guys with answers that land them on the positive side of your list, eliminate much of the guesswork. When you know, while still dating, what a man thinks about your ideas and how he will react to likeminded ideas in the future, it means you have some idea as to what you can expect from him. It puts you on the same level with men who are out looking for a woman, who may be just like you . . . and guys *are* looking too. When you repeat-date men who enjoy and share your views and aspirations, you assure yourself a wide playing field. Your list gives you a range of people to safely fall in love with. Its safe because you can feel his love in his support. It is safe because the ambitions factor is about *us* not just him.

There will probably be other men before you find *HIM,* but *when* you do (not *if* you do) its going to be like everything you've ever imagined love can be, including long-lasting, workable, fulfilling, satisfying, fill in the blanks . . . for you both. The criteria is an open. No one need be prejudged! This methodology lifts off the social straightjacket that demands, "You've got to, should, shouldn't must, mustn't, no-no-no, can't, ought to, etc., etc.," along with other outdated conventions that are causing marriage failures.

You know what those customs and traditions are and you can employ them when you choose to or not, or only if they fit. Right now, however, *your* personal aspirations are the rule, and you and Fate are working your destiny together around your personal choices. Imagine the satisfaction of marrying a man who thinks your goals are as important as his are.

The path to a good marriage is like a journey. It begins, or ends, with the care, effort, fun and enjoyment you put into the first parts, which are your list and dating. The selection of dating partners is number two and the mixture of these efforts equals the quality within the resulting marriage.

Competition and Jealousy

Dip your hand into a bagful of problems and competition and jealousy will probably stick like super glue. (C&J) can be hard to deal with at any time in life. So if (C&J) is one of the plays you don't like in dating life, this is a method that can change your game. Its custom-designed for your own satisfaction. This plan is more fun than C&J. In this contest, there are no bets, no losers and no schemes. The HQ method mostly dismisses the contest part from your love story.

The groundwork is done. The quest (your list) will help you find opinions and get clarity, first in your own mind, then to learn how a date feels about your goals, with who and what you are, and who and what you plan to become.

You go out on a date, you play a little, laugh and dance, and then you sprinkle in some of your HQ, he answers. Do you like the answers he gave? You might ask for details on his opinions, but that's it! This answer is who he is, how he thinks, what he likes. If you like his responses, great. Consider the question and the method a success. Continue to date him.

Note: Do not make the mistake of assuming he will change. Also do not make the mistake in thinking that you can change him. He is who he is, DNA stays as is. Only person you can ever change is you, if you want to.

So, if his answers prompt you to start thinking, "Error,

Error, back away!" You may also consider the question and the method a success.

Really, it is that easy. The date is over. You had a good time, everything is fine but you let him go! You let him go because you have nothing in common with him. Your 'there place' is not where he wants to be. He's not with you on your goals, he's not on with your ambitions, your dreams, poof, nothing! No support for what is important in your life.

You can be sure he will not be your date again! Not because he is a bad guy, but because he is not for you. Your core ideals conflict or are opposite to his . . . and so . . . you needn't care if he becomes someone else's perfect date. That's how the C&J action stops being a game maneuver. These are the facts! When you let him go for these reasons, you force out the competition & jealousy ingredient that makes so many feel like dating is a competitive sport.

Congratulate yourself! You have made a big, important step! Your HQ helped you learn that he's not your dream date. His plans are contrary to yours, and you know that because he didn't pass your Hard Questions test.

Note: Now and again, ask yourself, "If I didn't ask this question and get this answer, would I still be dating him?"

TWO YEARS! REALLY?

No doubt marriage will have prickly times. Yet better to live it tossing the ball back and forth between the two of you, laughing in celebration of your marriage, rather than dragging your vows like a bowling ball tethered to your ankle.

The HQ list and the Question & Answer duo, act together as a set up for success. This combo is like a self-styled, modern-day matchmaker in your head, where nobody looses.

As your dating develops into a relationship and moves into the 'for-sure couple' stage, the two year safety zone picks up the threads of your single lives, and intertwines them.

As this connection ripens, the interest, variety and intensity take on trust, confidence and form. This time is your trial union. The clock ticks no matter what . . . better to travel through it and find out at the end of the two years, time which will pass anyway, assured that you either belong together or not.

The two year dating period, is a free and easy fun zone between being single and being married. So as your awareness of each other expands with all the talking, walking, laughing, loving and growing, let this also be a time to loosen up and play with each others toys, a premarital celebration which engages your love as a long fun date as well as a lighthearted_possible betrothal. These two years are meant to acquaint ones intended with the family, role models, exchange ideas on marital methods, play together and explore life goals.

Experience is key to a wise choice. Indeed, this time period is the best, most compatible option for shaping your marriage before it begins. A business friend told me about the five P's: Prior Planning Prevents Poor Performance. The five P's apply to marriage as well.

Such an engagement length may result in marriage or the attraction may fall apart, but this period of familiarity tends to eliminate most divorces as the two year time span is the point around which a couple decides how . . . what . . . if and . . . why to spend their lives together.

If you realize its not going work, the break up means you loose some clock time and a partner possibility. Better to start with the two years, learn you don't fit together sooner rather than later, gather up your experiences and move on. Divorce rates are built on the alternative.

The sweet earthy paradise that is the love of your life, the man of your dreams, that perfect Mr. Him is one of the brightest stars that will ever swoosh into your life. Ask anyone married for a long time to *that guy*, who is still the man of her dreams, and she will certainly confirm it. This practice helps you find the type of man who would be a desirable marriage partner, then places a happy marriage easily within reach.

Life doesn't come with a guarantee, however, following these methods, gives some control over the success meter. Why? Because as Cinderella you get to determine the hopes and dreams you want to pursue; which Prince is the most desirable marriage partner; make plans together to shape your aspirations and his . . . and; whether you want to buy or rent your castle.

These pages are abridged from a book Hines-Jurgens is writing, illustrating how people handle life problems and goal achievement. In it she lays out various short story experiences, positive and negative. These accounts compose the 25 chapters. The stories are interspersed with operable practices readers can relate to, based on the above-described three-point plan.

**Statistics: Begin with census numbers from 1970s onward. Census indicate many years where half the marriages in the United States end in divorce. The 'system,' as is, no longer works for people, and the numbers prove it. * (site divorce stats)*

**Statistics (include census from 1970 onward) indicate over half the marriages in the United States end in divorce.*

***

Lois Hendricks

Lois was raised as a 'preacher's kid' in a small coal-mining town in Pennsylvania. She later migrated to Southern California where she worked and rubbed elbows with others at Desilu.

Writing has always been her passion and she loves to live in the world of fiction. Lois has published numerous poems and short stories. Also among her achievements is a novel she published called ***Edge of the Woods.***

ARE YOU LISTENING TO ME, HOWIE?

As he removed the old balcony floor boards Howie could hear Maude's shrill voice drifting out through the slightly open sliding door. The porch light shone on his small, slim hand gripping the hammer. He relaxed and scratched his bald head, then stood and walked to the railing.

The house of their closest neighbor, situated high on the cliffs and outlined by the glow of the moon, was dark. Below Howie could hear the waves from Big Sur crashing against the cliffs. Looking back at his small porch light he watched several moths flying around the light.

Howie went back to work, carefully removing the nails and stacking the used boards at the side of the balcony. He gazed down through the gaping hole in the floor. The moon glistened on the wet, jagged rocks far below. As Howie placed the first board in place he hummed, then hammered.

Suddenly the sliding glass door slid all the way open.

A tall, heavy-set woman draped in a bright blue, flowing robe and blue bedroom slippers stood in the doorway. "Howie, are you listening to me?"

"What, dear?" Howie's face contorted into a frown.

"Stop hammering. Are you still fixing that floor? It's getting late. We could pay someone to do that. After all you're a stress engineer, not a carpenter."

"I'm almost done, dear."

"I can't see why you feel the need to finish this before the neighbors return tomorrow from vacation. I'm sure they wouldn't mind a little pounding. Besides, I don't think they can hear the noise from up there."

"But dear, I don't like to bother anyone--"

"Oh, never mind, Howie," she snapped brusquely and patted her thick, permed hair. "Really...you're such a mouse, but I suppose I should be grateful you found those rotting boards in the balcony floor."

"Thank you, dear, I--"

"Eeek!! These awful bugs." Maude chased a moth away from her face, then ducked into the house. She slammed the sliding door shut, cutting off her words.

Howie kept hammering as a wisp of his wife's odd-smelling perfume drifted to him.

* * *

The next morning Howie knotted his dark brown tie and entered his and Maude's well-lit, airy kitchen.

Maude stood at the sink with her back to him. "Be sure to take your suit to the cleaners today, Howie." She stared at him. "Are you listening to me?"

"Yes, dear."

"Well, I certainly hope so," she snapped as she placed a bowl of oatmeal on the table.

He sat down and looked at the bowl of oatmeal sitting on the table and wrinkled up his nose. He thought longingly of the bacon and eggs they used to have for breakfast until Maude decided they needed to diet.

Howie shut his eyes. He could almost taste the bacon. *Why do I have to cut back? My doctor said I'm too thin. I'm tired of slipping to the refrigerator late at night after Maude starts snoring.* He opened his eyes. Anger stirred inside him, but he said nothing as usual.

"Howie, do you remember Jonathan Rubenstein?" Maude asked abruptly.

Howie dropped his spoon. "Who, dear?"

Maude sat down across from Howie. The chair squeaked. "You know that multi-millionaire who used to work for the same company you do. We met him, a man in his late sixties, and his wife at a party the company gave two years ago." Maude made a disapproving face. "She was a young floozy. What was her name?" Maude stopped and plucked at her stored-up memories. Then her puffy facial features brightened. "Roxanne! That was it. She even bumped into us at the party and then took forever to apologize. I finally walked off."

Howie shook his head. "No...no dear, I can't say I remember them." He bent over his bowl of oatmeal.

"Oh, I might have known you wouldn't remember," Maude scoffed disdainfully. "Anyhow," Maude continued, "there was an article in the newspaper about Rubenstein."

She placed both elbows on the shiny mahogany table, cupped her chin in her hands and leaned toward Howie. The table creaked.

Lowering her voice she added, "They found him last night drowned in his own swimming pool! Can you imagine? That floozy of a wife, Roxanne, will probably spend all his money on the next man." Maude stared at Howie.

"Poor man," Howie said, gagging on a mouthful of oatmeal.

The shrill sound of the telephone interrupted the silence.

Pushing herself up from her seat Maude walked to the phone. Her back was to Howie.

Howie quickly jumped up and emptied the remainder of his oatmeal down the disposal, then sat down again.

After Maude hung up she looked at the clock. "You better go, Howie," she snapped. "You'll be late. Don't just sit there."

"I have ten minutes yet," Howie stammered.

"Get going," she yelled.

Howie stood and headed toward the front door.

"Wait," Maude said behind him, "don't forget your hat and umbrella."

"But, dear--"

"But, nothing! It looks like rain. Now hurry up. You don't want to be late for work." Her hand was on his shoulder, pushing him out the door.

He grabbed his hat from the hook. As he tried to turn in her grasp he inhaled her odd scent again. He shifted his briefcase to the other hand to take the black umbrella she extended. He looked at Maude.

"Yes?" she asked. "For Heavens' sake what is it now? I can't stand here all day."

"You...you can sit out on the balcony again, dear. It's safe. I finished last night after you went to bed."

"Good. Now get going." Maude turned abruptly and hurried

back inside the house, slamming the door shut.

Howie glanced up at the sunny skies, then at the umbrella in his hand. As he walked down the sidewalk bordered by flowers, he frowned.

Once he slid behind the wheel he smiled.

He arrived in the bustling city and drove down a four-lane street divided by an island, careful to stop for all the red lights, bikes and pedestrians. A car in the lane to his left suddenly cut in front of him. Howie slammed on the brakes. For the first time in years of driving the irritation he felt from thoughtless drivers was too much. He honked.

A feeling of release came over him, a freedom he had not experienced since he'd married Maude, a wealthy widow, some twenty years earlier.

He parked at his place of work, reached into the back seat for his umbrella, then went inside and up on the elevator. As he passed his co-workers in the large front office he nodded 'Good Morning' only to those who nodded first.

Once inside his closet-size office he sat down. With a sigh he reached for the books and folders on his desk that he'd come to hate. He made some notes on a notepad.

At coffee break voices drifted back through his open door. Glancing out the glass partition in the top half of his office wall Howie saw the other employees gather around the coffee pot. Albert rushed over to them, his Adam's apple bobbing up and down in his gangly neck as he leaned into his group of co-workers and whispered. The others huddled around him, then they stared toward Howie's office, their faces grim.

Several of them, led by Albert, started Howie's way.

Howie stood up. His palms were wet.

Albert opened Howie's office door. The others crowded around. Some clasped their hands together. One woman was crying softly.

"Howie," Albert began, "we just had a phone call. Your wife...well, there was an accident and it looks like--"

Howie came around his desk. His hand rested on the surface. "Yes?"

Albert's voice dropped. "She's gone. I'm sorry."

Two of the women gathered around Howie. They placed their hands comfortingly on his arms and looked into his face.

Howie forced himself to stand still.

The men nodded. One of the women urged, "Sit down, Howie. You look like you're going to faint."

"I'll be okay." He let them lead him to a chair where he sat down. "What...what happened?"

"She was on the balcony. The floor gave way and she must have fallen."

"Oh, God." Howie's face contorted as he began to sob. He dropped his head into his hands. He felt someone's arm slip around him.

"The neighbors heard her screaming and called the police. Apparently she was alone in the house."

"Where is...she?"

"The ambulance took her away a few minutes ago."

When Howie looked up, tears wetting his face, he said, "I...I must leave...go to her..."

"Do you want us to do anything?" Albert asked. "Maybe one of us should go with you."

"Thanks, but no, I'll be okay." Slowly Howie stood, shook his head to all their questions and went to a corner of the room. After taking his hat and umbrella off the coat rack he shuffled out the door into the big office. Behind him he heard his co-workers whispering.

"Poor man, he was so devoted to his wife."

"He did whatever she said."

"They had such a nice life together...just the two of them."

Howie closed the outside office door softly behind him and walked down the hall.

When the elevator doors opened he stepped inside, found himself alone, and pushed the button for the main floor. Once the doors closed he looked at the umbrella in his hand which Maude had forced him to bring to work. In a surge of anger tinged with freedom he slammed the umbrella into the corner. Removing his hat he sent it twirling to land on top of the umbrella. With a deep sigh and smile he removed his tie and stuffed that into a pocket, then opened his top shirt button. Just before the doors wheezed open he removed his brown coat and draped it over his arm.

He stepped out, went around the corner to a large potted plant and pulled out his cell phone. Humming softly he dialed a number.

"Hello?" a woman said in a sultry tone.

"Roxanne, sweetheart, this is Howard." He cleared his throat. "That matter we had scheduled for today is taken care of. You've been so patient. We both have. I'll see you later today at the usual place." His smile was so wide he thought his face would split. "We have to be careful for a while until I collect her insurance money, then I'll quit my job. After that we can travel. I don't have to leave you early tonight or any other night...from now on."

***

One Has Curls

At my school there are lots of girls
But one of them has all these curls.
Some girls are great and some are not.
This curly-haired one ain't so hot.
Her nose is flat, her hair is gold
And she's a real mean nine-year old.
She thinks she's great and oh so smart
Here's a drawing of her in art!
Last day of school she sent this note.
I opened it. Here's what she wrote.
"I think you're cute and very kind,
I watch you always from behind,
How 'bout a snack with me today
At recess 'fore we run and play?"
With a smile she passed me candy
I ate some. Sure tasted dandy.
After school I hauled her books
You should have seen the funny looks
And lots of snick'ring from the guys.
But I don't care...they're not so wise.
They followed us out to her bus
And all those geeks just stared at us.
Angie stepped up and gave me fruit.
I smiled at her...you know, she's cute
Yes, summer's here with all the fun,
But now I know I'll miss someone!!

RUNNING AWAY

Mom wanted me to make my bed,
And straighten up my room each day,
'Then throw out all the trash,' she said.
Enough's enough...I ran away.
I didn't bring a thing to eat.
And mom won't let me cross the street
Before too long it'll sure be dark
And yes, Siree, it's gonna rain.
Did you hear thunder from the park?
My stomach's starting to complain.
I'm hungry. I want my dinner
I'm cold now and getting thinner.
If I should turn and go right back
I bet my mom will warm my hide.
She's bound to give me one good whack,
But...she deserves another try
And that good food she cooks is great!
So if I run, I won't be late!

FOOTPRINTS

We walked behind daddy today,
Through muddy grass along the way.
His boots left marks so long and wide,
That mine looked really small beside.
I sure felt bad to be so small
With daddy big and really tall.
And then I got a great surprise...
Kid brother's prints were half my size!

WHO WANTS TO BE A NERD?

Hey, when your mom wants you to work
Don't do a thing...don't be a jerk.
Just nod but don't you say a word
'Cause say, who wants to be a nerd?
Wait until you hear the phone ring.
Boy, that's when you can really swing.
Just take your ball, sneak out the door
For sure she'll talk an hour or more.
Now I came outside long ago
Because my mom will never know.
I like to do things nice and cool
And go by my own kind of rule.
Oh, oh, guess what, here comes my mom.
Now where on earth did she come from?
Hey, wait, mom, wait, don't spank me--ow!
Yes, ma'am, I'll do my jobs right now!

MY PET

I took my pet frog with me today
To see what the kids at school would say.
When I placed him on my desk with care
He jumped and landed in Susie's hair.
She screamed.
I beamed.
But then that mean old teacher, Miss Mear,
Came running back and yelled in my ear.
The kids laughed while spots hopped out the door
And I never saw him any more.
I sighed,
Then cried.
For awhile I missed my old buddy
But know he's happy where it's muddy.
And now that's okay 'cause I got Jake.
I'll take him tomorrow...my pet snake!

Louise Watkins

C. L. WOODHAMS aka
LOUISE WATKINS

Louise Watkins chose her grandmother's maiden name as her pen name, thinking it sounded like an English mystery writer. In order to get published in her grandmother's day, women had to use only their initials so that the editors would think they were men.

Louise is a past president of Southwest Manuscripters currently living in North County, San Diego. She is active there in Publishers and Writers of San Diego, Read Local San Diego and the North County Writers Bloc. She has served as a judge for the San Diego Book Awards.

Louise is actively soliciting agents for her suspense novel, *The Outreach Committee*, and is in the umpteenth rewrite of a mystery novel, *Widow's Walk*. Her works have appeared in several anthologies, news papers and newsletters. Her collection of short mysteries, *Sweet Justice* is available in print and on Kindle from Amazon.

Visit Louise at her website, ***clwoodhams.com,*** comment on her posts at womenbreakfreefromabuse.wordpress.com, or e-mail her at ***clw@clwoodhams.com.***

OUTREACH EXPRESS: WOMEN BREAKING FROM ABUSE

Blog Excerpts

(womenbreakfreefromabuse.wordpress.com)

BY C. L. WOODHAMS

Men's Abuse Of Women: What Are Its Origins?

Today we hear more and more about the abuse of women in relationships: in families that are rich and poor, famous and unknown, old and young. Where did it all start? Why does it still continue in spite of our public discussions of it? Is it because society considers women inferior? Let's think about these rhetorical questions.

When I was a child, we laughed at cartoons of a cave man dragging "his" woman by her hair to his cave. Was our enjoyment of this comic the beginning of our acceptance of the inferior status of women in our society—and does the belief that women are inferior go that far back in time? *My* answer is yes.

In many ancient civilizations, women were considered chattel. Unfortunately, the same is true of many societies today. Women are "owned" by their fathers and then their husbands. A woman's family must provide a dowry so that she becomes "worthy" of becoming a gentleman's wife. This ownership gives the father in Texas the right to beat his daughter with a belt to teach her a lesson. It gave the Middle Eastern family in Canada the moral or religious right to murder their teen daughters because they were assuming "Western ways."

In the United States, we think of ourselves as champions of equality between the sexes. But there is a mountain of evidence that shows that we are far from that goal:

- Several of our major religions have no women in their management hierarchy.
- Our armed forces do not permit women to serve in front-line combat zones.

- A bank may choose not to consider a woman's income in its decision on whether to approve a mortgage loan, because she could become pregnant and leave the workforce.
- Women earn thirty percent less than men doing the same job.

In my lifetime, a female student was made fun of by a college engineering professor, in front of the entire class, for wanting to enter a "man's" occupation. She left engineering and become a pharmacist.

I was once told by my boss that I could not go on a business trip with men; fortunately, the project manager from another department disagreed and I did go.

Clearly we have a long way to go on the equality front.

The question becomes: Is a woman's lower place in society the source of spousal abuse?

Maybe.

Why do men abuse women?

The answer is *control.*

My teen friends and I used to talk about how romantic it was when a boy wanted to be alone with his one and only, shutting out her friends and family. In reality, if this isolation continued beyond the first bloom of love, our hero was showing one of the first signs of his *need* to control the relationship.

A control that *could* escalate into physical violence when his woman did not meet his every whim, or when he could not solve the problems he encountered in the outside world.

It's especially abhorrent when one person feels the need to control the marriage. Isn't marriage a partnership? In a business partnership, the duties are divided according to each partner's capabilities and knowledge. Why isn't it so in many marriages?

Grocery-shopping couples provide examples of the continuum of control in a relationship. She timidly asks if he'd like tomatoes in his salad; she receives a demeaning stare and no answer. She chooses a package of fish; he grabs it and throws it back into the display, selecting an identical one to put in the shopping cart. She says, "Look, there's my favorite candy" reaching for the box. He slaps her hand away.

The person in power is always the one to abuse. But if one already has power, there should be no need to prove it. But there *is* a need to maintain the power.

So the male abuser plays on and perpetuates a woman's already-instilled feeling of inferiority. Thus he leads her into accepting her lower status and the abuse as natural and deserved.

The controller at the super market will stand by with a wad of money in a gold clip while his wife pulls out a calculator and counts pennies in the bottom of her purse to make sure she has enough in the household account he's given her to buy the groceries. He'll point to another woman who is dressed as though going to church. "Why don't *you* look like that when you go out with me? *Look* at you—you look like you've been washing floors."

Why do these men feel a need to control?

The need to control is driven by fear.

Perhaps a man's belief that he *should* be superior leads to abuse when he becomes afraid that he is not.

A man who fears he is losing control becomes violent. Because of this, filing an injunction against an abuser while still in the home may be a fatal move for the abused woman.

Why don't women learn? Why don't they see the red flags of abuse and go running the other direction?

One reason that abuse is perpetuated may be because it is never discussed with children during their formative years.

In my family, we didn't discuss unhappy things. I was grown before I learned that a favorite cousin's husband, whom I adored, disappeared from the family circle when I was ten because his wife and child escaped to her parents' home battered and bruised.

If young girls could be made to understand that even a seemingly nice, charismatic guy is capable of abuse —and that abuse is *wrong*—that would have a positive impact.

Today, many younger men actively participate in childcare and household chores, instead of sitting in front of the TV while their working wives clean the house and put the children to bed. Many men would never abuse any woman. But is men's abuse of women ending?

No.

We as a society have to find a solution to this ongoing blight, and a way to protect the abused from the abuser.

The solution in my suspense novel, *The Outreach Committee*, fights violence with violence. It rids society of the abusers, but it does not solve the underlying problem.

Do you have a solution? We all will benefit from your input.

Peace, CLW

Is it an Argument or Verbal Abuse?

No one of us would expect that a relationship could bloom without disagreements. Talking out your divergent views on a subject adds to your understanding of your partner and his appreciation of you.

However good for the marriage these discussions may be, they should be true disagreements between equals, not verbal abuse.

How can you tell the difference? Consider this:

- An argument may be loud, but it's in private. An abusive accusation often takes place in front of others.
- In an argument each person is respectful of the other's opinion or view and gives them time to express it. In verbal abuse, only the abuser's feelings, anger, and reasoning are projected. The abused is expected to remain silent and agree.
- The abuser assumes and expects his partner to recognize that he is always right, no matter his knowledge or expertise.

- An argument discusses concrete issues. It is not one person berating the other over even the most insignificant of faults.
- An argument discusses only the immediate disagreement, not a myriad of complaints from times past.
- An argument is words only. Verbal abuse escalates from words to hitting, or it may start with hitting.
- In an argument, words fly but not dishes or the abused person's belongings.
- Arguing fair means you can say to him, "Let's table this until we cool off." And he respects it.
- Arguing means the partners can agree to disagree after a discussion of the issue and still respect each other.
- Arguing ends in love. Verbal abuse ends in hate.

Do you have other definitions? We all will benefit from your input.

Peace, CLW

What Do Friends Know? What Should They Do?

I remember walking with a newlywed co-worker. She and her husband both worked with us and had met at work. She seemed glowingly happy with her marriage. I commented on a three inch bruise on her upper arm. She blushed and said, "I get a little violent during ... Oh never mind." We walked, on discussing work. I have often wondered if she was abused. Was she into rough sex? No matter, I should have followed up at a later time.

A friend who *was* abused by her first husband, years ago, told me she'd go to work with bruising up and down her arms. She found it difficult to hide the splotches. No one said a word to her about the cause of the ugly marks, until she had divorced.

I hope we are different today. Another friend who takes aspirin for her heart and bruises easily, often sports black and blue wrists. Just the slightest bump when removing clothes from the washer or pulling off a Band-Aid turns her arms deep purple. Friends, both men and women, have asked about the ugly bruises. She's open about them and their cause. However, a woman in an abusive relationship often believes her abuser when he says, "It's your fault that I hit you." She may be hurting but too embarrassed to confess that she caused the fight that bruised her.

We owe our abused friends a dedication that makes us reach out and help. In helping a friend who is in trouble we are also showing the proper way to behave in a loving friendship.

What would you do? Act as a wailing wall? Help her physically break free? Find her a place to live? Offer her money or find her a job? Research shelters for her? All of the above? Or other? We all need to think about it, decide what to do. Then, we'll be prepared when the situation arises.

I'd like to hear what you have done to help a woman break free.

Peace, CLW

The Children Know

She told me that her children didn't know their father was abusing their mother until they were teens and caught him at it. Then, they told their father that they would "beat him up" if he ever hit their mother again. He stopped.

I would wager that the children *did* know. No home's walls are thick enough to barrier angry words or an involuntary cry of pain. Children soak up all kinds of information by observing their parents. Something they do constantly. Mom's tear stained face tells them she's lying even when she says she had a silly accident. Dad's scowl each time he looks at their mother tells them something is going on.

Whether or not you feel the children know you are being abused, you *must* put them first. First before your fear of the future if you leave; first before you risk his following you; first before your belief that you are not qualified to find work.

If you don't leave: the violence could escalate to the children; your son will learn all the wrong ways to treat a woman or become a bully to everyone around him. If you stay: your daughter learns that a controlling angry man is normal husband material; she doesn't have a chance to learn that gentle caring men are the ultimate mates.

Your children *could be* one avenue for coping with your husband's abuse. Use their welfare to convince him you need to leave the home for short periods. He may object, but probably can't justify to himself making you stop what you're doing if it benefits his children. Consider working to gain money for their college, or volunteering in your child's classroom, or working with the PTA to collect funds for a new computer lab.

You may not be ready to break away completely, but these activities will benefit you and your children. You *need* to get out for a while, every day if possible. Making friends with coworkers or other volunteers will provide you a stash of friends to whom you can confess your abuse. They may be the very ones who will help you break free.

If you've escaped or coped well, what's your experience? We'd like to hear from you.

Peace, CLW

How Do You Know He'll Be Abusive? What Clues Does He Give You?

When I started talking about my new blog, women came to me to reveal for the first time that they had been, or were still in, an abusive relationship. These women all had one comment in common. They did not know that their husbands were abusive until after they married. "He was so sweet and loving before." This was then followed by something similar to: "I felt betrayed when he started hitting me, and wondered what warning signs I'd missed during our courtship."

I'll mention some potential warning signs, but I'd appreciate your writing and telling me those signs which you know, in retrospect, that you ignored.

- He had a great sense of humor, but his jokes were often at my expense, especially in front of others.
- He always wanted to be doing something. Sitting around and talking about our relationship or just snuggling wasn't on his action list.
- He'd promise to do something I wanted to do, but then he'd "forget" and go off with this buddies. Blame me for getting angry.
- Our relationship was always about him: his schedule, his ideas, and his friends.
- He was polite to my family, but made fun of them behind their back.
- My friends were "silly" or "immature" or he didn't like them.
- He wanted me all to himself: no double dating or going to *my* friends' parties.
- He was irrationally upset if I talked to other men.
- My clothes embarrassed him because they weren't what the other girls in his crowd (or town) were wearing.

- When I said I needed to write, pursue a hobby, or spend time with my family, he accused me of wanting to break off the relationship.
- He was angry a lot of the time. He'd say his anger was caused by others, often me. If he wasn't angry he was unhappy.
- He didn't take responsibility for bad things that happened to him. He blamed others.
- He was unsure of himself, needed constant praise from me. I was expected to compliment him on his successes, but he ignored mine.
- He didn't get along with his co-workers.

Sound familiar? Are there other warning signs you can contribute? If you know girls of dating age, please discuss these and your ideas with them.

Peace, CLW

Mary Brenneman, M.D.

Education:

University of Toronto, Ontario, Degree – M.D. 6/1947; University of Pittsburg, PA, Degree – MA Public Health in Maternal Child & Health 6/1958; Rotating Intern, Western PA Hospital, 7/1947-1948; Pediatric Resident I Western PA Hospital, Pittsburg 7/1949-6/1950; Psychiatry Resident 1, 2, 3 Camarillo State Hospital 7/1968-6/1971.

Work Affiliations:

Pediatrician, Pittsburg Public Health Dept. and B.G.G Vaccine Program 1950-1957; University of Pittsburg Pediatrics Clinical Instructor 1950-1957; Kaiser Hospital, Hollywood Pediatrician 1957-1958; Santa Monica Hospital Pediatrician 1961-1962; Camarillo State Hospital Psychiatrist 1968-1973. St. John of God Nursing Hospital Psychiatric Consultant 1963-1975; St. John's Hospital, Santa Monica L.A County Crisis, Day-Care Psychiatrist 1973-1975.

Other Medical and Scientific Societies and Activities Apart From Hospital:

Clinical Instructor in Pediatrics, UCLA 1957-1968; Member, American Psychiatric Association 1973-; Member, So. Cal. Psychiatric Society 1973-; Member, L.A. Society for Adolescent Psychiatry 1973-; Member, West Society for Scientific Study of Sex; Established Prolixin Clinic, St. John's Hosp. 1974-1975; School Physician, L.A. Board of Education 1962-1968; Psychiatric Director, Penny Lane Institution for Teen Age Emotionally Handicapped, Sepulveda 1975-; 5 yeah Jungian Analysis with Drs. Harold Store, Training analysis, Malcom Dana, Training Analyst and three years student of C.G. Jung Institute 1975-1978.

Honors:

1. Who's Who of American Women, Who's Who of America; 2. Chief, Research Grant for Moonwalker for Limb-Handicapped, U.C.L.A Medical Center From Children's Bureau, HEW, 1965,1966.

"In The Morning" won first place in a National writing competition through Southwest Manuscripters Club of Los Angeles in 2011.

IN THE MORNING

In the morning

I sit in the sun

At my kitchen table.

I look out at the yellow buttercups

Dotting the clover.

My hand feels the warmth of the sun

Streaming through the window

From ninety-three million miles away.

Is this enough to say

"There is a God who made it this way"?

--Mary Brenneman, MD
Feb. 8, 2010

Part of "Nature's Cycle" won Honorable Mention in a National Writing competition through Southwest Manuscripters Club of Los Angeles in 2011.

PART OF NATURE'S CYCLE

On a hill looking over the Ohio River,
In Sewickley (Indian for "running water"),
The school-girl trudged up to the wood
Beside the old cemetery
And its grey tumbling tombstones
With crumbling names and years in the 1800's.
Mary Lou roved the hillside to pick wild flowers:
Anemones spraying tiny pink lines
Delicate across the white petals,
And cool violets, plentiful bunches in the shade from poplars.

A handful of flowers would be given
To Laura, her mother, ever glad
To put them in water.
In Spring, sturdy yellow daffodils
With their long stems standing high—
Were offered proudly from daughter to mother.

Mary Lou, one of five daughters,
Was seldom missed at home
When she jaunted off,
Free as a bird
To be part of Nature's cycle,
Then return home to the nest.

--Mary Brenneman, M.D.
March 13, 2001

MaryAnn M. Butterfield

I fell in love with the printed word at an early age; possibly because I had "printer's ink in my veins," as Dad used to say. Besides working for a publisher of fine leather-covered books, he had been a printer on a small weekly paper and I would sit in rapt attention whenever he spoke about how "...in the 'old' days we did a little bit of everything...digging up news items, taking stories over the phone, selling advertising and collecting bills."

When I showed an interest in writing, and after I'd published a number of non-fiction pieces, my Dad gifted me with a scrapbook of hundreds of columns written by Sarah DeWolfe Webster Milton, my Great-Grandmother, and a columnist in the mid-1800s for ***The Boston Globe*** and other Boston newspapers. Her passion inflamed my passion—it *was* in my blood!

At present, I am working on several children's chapter books and "tween" stories, along with a non-fiction biography. From this work, I derive the same satisfaction and happiness I believe my Dad and Great-Grandmother did when their written drafts were put into print and rolled off the presses. It is my dream that our one-hundred-sixty-two-year legacy of writing and loving the printed word will continue in our family for generations to come.

MY TOO BIG NOSE

Oh God, Andy's coming this way. That's him at the end of the hallway. He's the last person I want to see right now. Just my stupid luck! Nothing ever goes right for me.

I grab my stuffed backpack from Locker Eight (he has Locker Ten) and slam the metal door closed with my elbow. It bounces back open. This time I shove the door with my sweaty hand, almost dropping my notebooks. Thankfully, the lock catches.

"Crystal. . ." Andy's voice calls after me, but I pretend not to hear and run down the hall in the opposite direction.

This started out as a perfectly good week. I hung around football practice every afternoon pretending to wait for my brother. What I wanted was for his friend Andy to notice me and ask me to the Festival Dance!

On Monday, Andy asked, "Hi, waiting for your bro?" and I said, "Yes, we walk home together a lot." How dumb is that! Then each day after practice, I'd wait, and he'd come over and talk to me about stuff that happened in school. It was real nice. But, I could kind of feel like today was the day he was going to ask me about the dance.

Now what do I do? To begin with, I have a *huge* nose which I hate! To make matters worse, I now have a colossal red zit sitting center stage and rising every hour like Mt. Olympus. I only wish I hadn't tried to pick it last night. I should have waited just a little longer, but noooooooo, instead I just had to squeeze it. How'd I know the swelling would be there this morning. . .worse than ever?

Besides, how could you *not* squeeze an enormous whitehead sitting there like a beacon on a lighthouse? I don't even need a mirror. I have to look across it when I shift my eyes left or right! How gross. I should have pretended I'd gotten stung by a bee and put a Band-Aid on it!

Facing people in class and at practice was bad enough, but I don't want anyone else to see me . . .or this nose. My very best friend, Ginny, passed in my English Lit homework so I wouldn't have to walk to the front of the class. Thank goodness she can keep a secret.

I've kept running to stay ahead of Andy's schedule, and to get home as fast as I can to beat my brother. It's just my crappy luck that Andy is one of Matt's best friends and a teammate. Aaggggh!

My heart pounds as I run and I swear the zit is pulsing in rhythm to it. I make it home in record time and throw my knapsack on the bed. I race to the bathroom and switch on the light, keeping my eyes closed until after I turn to face the mirror. I take a peek.

Oh Gaaaaaawd, it's worse than ever on my sweaty red face. I look like a clown. I start bawling like a baby and the tears sting my eyes, making them red. My nose starts to run. I grab a tissue and blow angrily. Of course I make it bleed. Noooooooooo, I can't deal with this, I yell at my image. Why did I have to be born with this nose? I hate it!

I hear the front door slam. "Is that you, Matt?" I call out.

"Yeah, like who else would it be?"

"Would you call Mom and let her know we're home. I called yesterday."

"I've got stuff to do."

"Come on. Pleassssse?"

"Oh all right. Geeze, why do you have to make it such a big deal?"

Brothers! It's like pulling teeth to get them to do anything. He wouldn't understand that I can't bear to talk or see anyone right now, including him. I turn off my cell phone and put it in my desk.

Even with the pillow over my head, I hear the garage door rumble open. My parents carpool together and are home from work. That means they'll be checking in on me and Mom will want to talk about my faaaaaabulous day. No way! I duck into the shower and turn on the water just as I hear the knock on my door. "I'm in the shower, Mom."

"Okay, Darling. Don't be long. I picked up some barbeque and dinner will be ready soon."

Ha, this is one time I'm not going to sit at the table and have them all gawking at my nose. The warm water hitting my head and cascading down my body feels sooooooooo good. I wish I could swirl down the drain with the soap bubbles. How long do big zits last? If my nose weren't so big, it wouldn't look so bad. Maybe I can talk Dad into letting me get a nose job when I'm 18. A lot of girls do it, but I'm supposed to be proud of my heritage. . .and a lot of French people have the same shape nose, blah, blah, blah!

I step out of the shower, and avoid looking into the mirror as I towel off. I grab my pimple cream from the cabinet, throw on some old sweats and sit on the bed. By closing one eye, I can use the other to focus on the object of my misery. The nasty red zit looms before me as I cover it with the pimple cream. I now have a white nose, but that's better than before. I'm dead. I'll have this for a month.

A rap on the door startles me. "Dinner's ready," Dad announces.

I can smell the barbeque Mom's warmed up and suddenly I'm starving. "Okay. Be right there." I sprint back to the bathroom, comb my damp hair into a ponytail, and peel open a Band-Aid. So what if I look goofy.

Dad doesn't even notice the Band-Aid, but I can tell Mom is curious. She'll wait until later to ask, but I'll bet you a dollar Matt will say something any minute now. He's giving me "the look."

"So, why the Band-Aid on your nose Crys?" Matt asks, as if on cue.

"It's none of your business."

He shrugs. "Hey, only asking." A broad grin sweeps his face.

"Did you injure your nose, Crystal," Dad asks, cocking his head back and examining me through his bifocals.

"It's nothing, Dad. Just a little bump and I put some stuff on it." I glare at Matt.

"So it's just a pimple then?" Dad continues.

"Please! That isn't a dinner-time topic," Mom cuts in, "Let's change the subject."

I thank Mom under my breath, but I'm gonna kill Matt when I get him alone. He can be so nice one minute and so stupid the next.

Dad says, "Love the barbeque, Mother." Matt and I agree and Mom is pleased to talk about the new place she found around the corner.

It was delicious, and almost made it worth putting up with Matt, but I can't wait until dinner is over so I can leave the table.

It's my turn to load the dishwasher. I wipe the counter, grab a bottle of water and head back to my bedroom.

"Crys," my brother calls from his room. "Come 'ere."

"I'm busy."

"Okay, then don't say I didn't try to tell you."

"Tell me what?"

"Well come here and you'll find out."

He is so exasperating. Usually I want to hear what he has to say, but tonight I'm not in the mood for any funny stuff. This had better be good or he's really in for it. I stomp into his room. "I'm here! What is it?" I ask, flopping on to his bed.

Matt is at his desk and swivels the chair around to face me. Leaning forward, he braces his elbows on his knees and clasps his hands together. His brow furrows and I actually believe he wants a serious conversation.

"So what's up with you?" He asks in his I'm-soooo-your-big-brother-voice, even though he's only twelve-and-one-half months older than I am.

"What do you mean, 'What's up' with me?" I try to glare at him, but it is useless, given how miserable I feel.

"I heard from one of the guys that Andy was trying to ask you to the Festival Dance next week and you blew him off today."

"I did NOT blow him off."

"He said you did."

"Who said I did? I didn't even talk to Andy today," I huff, feeling guilty. I'm not about to explain myself; besides, I hadn't meant to be rude. I just didn't want Andy to see my nose.

"Doesn't matter," Matt continued in his big-brother way, "But, I know Andy wants to take you and you should give him a chance. He's one of the good guys. If he asked, would you go with him?"

I nodded a slow yes. "Matt, I wasn't trying to blow him off, but, like he's never going to ask me while I look like this."

"Like what?" he asks, straightening up.

"Matt," I say, raising my voice to get through to him, "Take a good look!" I whip off the Band-Aid and expose the pimple on the end of my nose. "Go ahead. Laugh if you want. I don't care.

"So you gotta zit? What's the big deal? We all get zits and we all get over them."

Matt might be a year older than I am, but he's a guy and sometimes guys just don't get it. "On my BIG nose, *everything* looks worse than on anybody else," I wail. "It isn't JUST a zit. This thing has taken over my nose. I look horrible."

"Jeeze, Chrys, you're such a drama queen. You don't have a big nose and *that* zit isn't *that* big!"

"I am not. And you aren't helping things." I flounce out of his room eager to be alone in the comfort of my room.

I don't know whether to feel really great that Matt told Andy he wants to take me to the dance, or really bad 'cuz Andy must have known I heard him call to me at school. I'm so busted and so embarrassed. I slather pimple cream all over my nose and go to bed! Thank goodness tomorrow is Saturday.

In the morning my zit looks a little better. Maybe. I'm really trying not to pick it again. Using a hand mirror, I check the side view before smearing on another gob of zit cream. Maybe if I put on my earphones and listen to my new download I'll stop thinking about it. Besides, I'm hungry just thinking about a leftover barbeque sandwich! I slip the I-Pod on to my belt and sing along as I dance out of the room.

WHAM! I collide with Andy in the hallway. With the headphones on, I never even heard him or the other guys come in the house. I freeze and put my hand up to cover my nose. Oh-my-God, I took off the Band-Aid when I put on the cream.

"Sorry, Crystal," Andy says, grabbing my arm to keep me from falling. "You okay?"

"Yeah, thanks," I stammer back. The words seem hallow in my ears. It's as though someone else were speaking in my voice. My pimple cream is now a white glob on Andy's letterman jacket and my glowing zit is totally exposed for the world to see. I can't breathe. I grab the headset off my head and feel the heat creeping up my neck. I know my face is turning beet red. Andy has to think I'm such a jerk.

Darn Matt anyway! He should have told me they were coming over. I duck to go around Andy, but the other guys are filling the hallway.

"Hey Crys, wait up," my brother hollers from his room. "Andy, go ahead and ask her now about the Festival Dance."

I see Andy's face flush. "Your brother is soooo smooth."

"Yeah!" Actually, my brother has the intelligence of a gnat. My heart is pounding and I'm gonna die on this very spot. By now, Andy's probably asked somebody else or wants to ask someone else!

"Ummm, Crystal," Andy says, still holding my arm. "Would you like to go to the Festival Dance with me next Saturday?"

Oh-my-God, he asked me. Now what do I do? "Ummm, I guess so." Again the words seem to come from somewhere else.

The guys behind him giggle and Andy tells them to keep quiet. Looking back at me he says, "Great! I'll call you when I'm not with these goons and we can set up the time and everything."

"Um, sure." I want to say something more, but my mind is blank.

"All right, then it's settled," Matt yells, shaking his head. "Now you can quit worrying about your nose."

I pull away from Andy. I am so furious, I forget *everything* except pounding Matt into oblivion! "I can't believe you just said that. You're such a jerk." I try to slug him, but Matt throws his arms up in defense.

"I'm just trying to help. You're the one who was worried about having a big nose!" His friends laugh and I remember where I am, who is watching, and want to disappear forever.

"You don't have a big nose, Crystal" Andy says, leaning closer to examine it. "And knock it off," he says to the other guys who are still snickering at my big football hero-brother cowering from my attempts to slug him.

Tears sting my eyes and I try to bolt, but Andy catches me by my shoulders and turns me around. Now the other guys in the hallway want a closer look. I am NEVER going to speak to my brother again.

"Really, you don't have a big nose, Crys," they say, peering at me like I'm a biology specimen. I feel myself being pulled into Matt's room and pushed in front of the mirror hanging above his dresser. One-by-one, the guys insist on comparing their noses to mine.

"This is a big nose," says one.

"Mine's bigger," says another.

"I've told her a hundred times that she doesn't have a big nose," asserts Matt, "But she *never* listens to me."

I stand frozen, staring into a mirror filled with faces. I look past the zit, and *see* my nose. . . maybe for the very first time ever.

One of the guys slips his finger under the tip of my nose and pushes it gently. "Look how funny you'd look with a smaller nose. You'd look like a Pekinese." They continue clowning in front of the mirror as Matt makes "woof woof" noises. I start laughing in spite of myself. Matt joins the group in front of the mirror.

"Sis, if you have a big nose, then what would you call mine?" He preens like a model, turning for a full profile against my profile.

Funny, I never thought about us having the *same* nose. I always thought Matt got the nice nose in the family. I look at his again, then back at mine. Mine *is* just like his, only. . . *smaller*. Smaller!

"Hey, guys, want some popcorn?" I ask, trying to break away from their scrutiny.

"Sure," they chorus.

I slip out of Matt's room, but stop in front of the hallway mirror for another quick peek. I really do have a nice nose. . . and the zit doesn't seem so big anymore. Plus I've got a great date for the Festival Dance. How perfect is that!

Now if only my boobs were just a little bit bigger. . .

The End

Maury Garnholz

Rocket engineer and science fiction writer Maury Garnholz's novel, ***Vision 2020: The 4 Horsemen at Bay,*** is coming out next year. He has been president of the Southwest Manuscripters in 1995-1996 and 2011. He was editor of ***The Write Stuff!*** for three long months. He is also a member of the Greater Los Angeles Writers Society (GLAWS), Surfwriters, the Writers Guild, Yuki Teiki Haiku Society, and the Southern California Haiku Study Group.

HAIKU

bands of marching cars
honk around loudly off-key
urban street music

two caterpillars
morph into bright butterflies
touch wingtips and soar

new year has embarked
overboard with old baggage
in with new matched set

(for *Southern California Haiku Study Group Anthology, 2012*)

swearing goals to keep
is later balanced by sounds
of oaths when broken

my plans all engraved
in stone this year to make sure
soon crumble to sand

again deja vu
new resolutions dissolve
intentions awry

one man, two women
what love connections exist
is this bliss or grief

(for *Cal Tech Poetry Journal, Wilson Fest, 2012, "Combinatorics for Poets")*

red queen, flamingo
kissing off like croquet balls
are they heads or tails
(ibid.)

schizo Möbius
his arguments are twisted
what side is he on

(***Scent of Rain,*** *Southern California Haiku Study Group, 2011)*

a gyre of lovers
linked in a tureen of kisses
fuel a heady whorl

haiku is precise
masters give all of the rules
a creative vise

orange and melon
circling the white breakfast plate
my wife greeting me

(Integral with painting by Terry Garnholz exhibited at UCLA and Chinatown, 2006)

a breath of cool air
wafts in from the noon ocean;
the umbrella luffs.

*(ibid. and **Scent of Rain,** Southern California Haiku Study Group, 2011)*

the thought of getting
by letting go together
may be worth a try

well-thumbed magazines
nervous coughs and fidgeting
doctor's waiting room

nosey voyeurs wake
aroma of love aroused
rutting woodland elk

St. Valentine's Day
in a not-saintly manner
tricky lovers' goal

all ways it's the spark
lovemaking starts with a kiss
that goes round and round

lovers learn too late
gorging on desserts too sweet
was it worth the ache

dining couple looks
will he, will she, the question
have dessert for two

she tries to be chaste
but finds it's better being
chased by lover's kiss
(Geppo, Yuki Teiki Society, 2011)

crows on black wires,
cawing in cacophony
music to our ears.

Pooh Bear loves his jar
It's like chasing butterflies
licking his honey

I drink it daily
your heartfelt chipped tea cup gift
Imperfect! It's me!

the hearth warms the hearts
coupled lovers are aglow
hot embers remain
(Geppo , Yuki Teiki Haiku Society, 2012)

TANKA

why do others save
such junk of little value
while I only store
those treasures I have acquired
for will-be-needed good use
(LAX Tankateers, 2011)

how to break the rule
that says you should break the rules
that's the first new rule
to-do, not-to-do, that's it
the question to be answered

so many years spent
filling our precious brains
then when almost full
the carefully sorted files
soon begin disappearing

at life's end I learn
the many plaques earned by me
are on the wrong walls
they're not displayed in my den
they're the ones inside my brain

my Rapunzle locked
in her mind's raveled castle
what thoughts tumble there?
her golden locks now silvered
blackened tangles thwart memories

HOT KISS OF DEATH

nakedly poolside
she gave her body to him
for his warm kisses
Apollo the seducer
deceived with too much of him
--maury for susan, 8/23/49 – 12/19/10
(died of melanoma)

PLARK PLACE

Oh I do so labor at resisting,
Buying with bricks of gold the chance to shirk;
Dreaming instead of delicious trysting,
I daily cringe at the dread sound of "work!"
Life's a game where early risers may not win,
So I blow in my ear a vision fey,
But the cosmic joker never sleeps in;
Ha, I'll beat him by sitting down to play.
Work alone chokes the heart; just play starves the frame;
A worldly jester named the Nobel quark;
A somber soldier spawned chess as a game;
Hence, I'll choose my path to fun 'n' funds as plark.*
PLAy and woRK can be joyfully mated,
And now Plark Place is where they're created.

**(PLAy + woRK = PLARK)*
(Sonnet, 1990.)
If Gell-Mann, in play,
can coin the quark,
then I, with my quirk,
can love my plark.

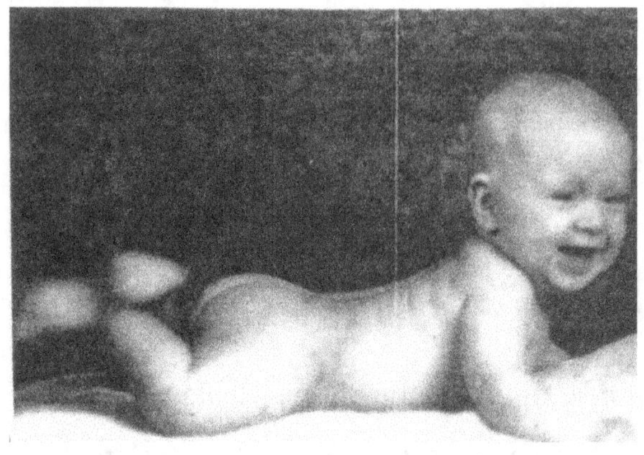

Baby Maury is so happy
After his bath he'll get his nappy
He has no reason to pout
For he just figured it out
He'll grow up as a novelist
And a rocket scientist. -- Yeah!

(The above offence was committed by the editor of this book. Oops!)

Michael Scanlon

The very first page of my biography is blank! Since I am a newcomer to writing Southwest Manu-scripters gave me a wonderful opportunity by offering me support, inspiration and a platform. I am trying out my brand new wings, hoping that I can fly.

As a child, I was labeled "un-teachable." At that time nobody knew about bi-polar or compulsive disorder, nor Asperger syndrome. The only way to cope with special-need children who didn't fit in and couldn't follow rules was to isolate them from the rest. They were labeled slow or retarded and they were often sent away to military schools or placed in inhuman psychiatric wards to be drugged or exposed to shock treatments. Special-need children then were condemned to a frightening, incomprehensive world, and to a sad and lonely life. Since I marched to a different drummer, people never had a chance to realize that my brain capacity equaled or even surpassed other children's. At my return from those dark places, my parents made me wash windows to make me feel useful. Since I didn't participate in living life fully, I became an observer. I spent a big portion of my adulthood caring for my Alzheimer-stricken mother, and for 17 years I've been managing a pop-star. However, I always had a secret love affair with words. I love them big, bold, beautiful and unusual. If a word cannot express my feeling, then I just go ahead and invent a new one. I love nature and beauty. In my heart I've always been a visionary, a dreamer and a poet.

THE METEORITE WATCHERS

It's oblivious to human eyes
And the mortal souls of this earth
But transparent to the chosen few
Its speed of light excels a million miles an hour
Exceeding the sound barrier
A translucent angel of mercy
Lights up the sky
As its fiery existence
Explodes into the Universe
With its cascading essence

Emotional meteorite
Traveling to galaxies
Journeying through
Solar storms
With fiery light forces
That radiate as one

Sunburst of emotion
Ejaculation of devotion
Envisioning anticipation
Wuthering heights of endearment
Sweet, impassionate embraces
In its mystical voyage of yester years

Meteorites orbiting around emerald
Volcanic eruptions of sapphire
And ruby red formations clusters
Are creating colorful sequences of sonic booms
Making its mark in metal tunes
As it resurrects its timeless
Uncharted course
Navigating its focus from the hemisphere.
Destinations unknown,
Automatic time set,
Charting our courses for our destiny.

Its enflamed eruptions
Consumes the universe
Flocking stargazers watch in awe
As it descends over the horizon
Flashpointing its fragments.

Feeding off the universe's nutrients
Creating one big vapor
Of galactic embrace
Its saga continues
In its epitaph.

Point of No Return

I passed the point of no return
Lost in your body,
Embedded in your soul
Intertwining your every thought
Maximizing your attitude
Accentuating and tantalizing
Your creative, imaginative aura
Reuniting of yester year
Through porcelain lovers'
Mirrored reflections
Traveling through
Unreachable magnitudes
Of dreamscapes
And all the wonders to be
Manifesting our golden bowl
Of translucent dreams to share.

The Vein of my Core.

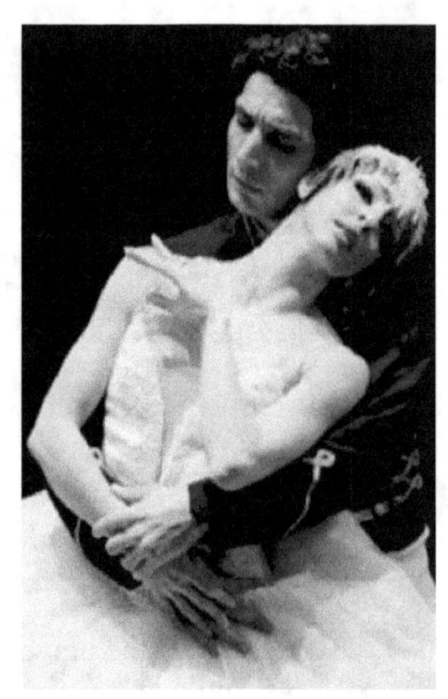

You are the vein of my core,
The center of my obsessiveness,
The entity of my
Creative imagination,
My never ending, interludeing
Vision of fantasy
A force shield around me
Relinquishing our turtle shells
With magnetic pull
Bestowed upon us
With dreams to share
Because we are home once again
In each other's arms
For an eternity:
We are one

Reflective Mirror

What You illustrate
I orchestrate
What You project
I reciprocate
What You assume
I generate back to You
In my reflective mirror

Twilight Reflections

We're sunset-catchers
And dream-masters
The sun melts
Dripping into the ocean
Like butter
Drenched in honey gold
And dissipates over the ocean's crest
Awaiting the mystery of deepening dusk
That brings cascading dreams
Of yesteryears.

We depart as dreamscapes navigate
Its course of chiseled memories
Filling our enlightened soles
Until dawn's early light
Surprises us
And unveils
Secret corridors
Of new beginnings,
Thundersoft and mellow.
And your thoughts are cream puffs
Sprinkling dust of amber sand.

Winter Dreams

Winter's dreamscapes,
Splashing seascapes
Unveiled fury
The forever changing
Array of colors
Absorbed by the ominous sky
Sucking up its breathtaking essence
Like a sponge
A sunset richness carved and sculpted
Of stars and golden mirrors
Of dreamscape's cascading seascapes
Echoing through the darkness of wondering clouds
Bringing joyousness suspended in time
Melting away the sadness like soft night winds
Warm and realizing.
Leather soft fingertip touches our souls
Melting ice-flowers
On the window panes
Of our minds
Refreshing memories
Unfolding spirits
As colored bright faces.
Satin velvet lace is
Igniting the
Glowing essence
Of love's golden force
Melting our porcelain
Creamy flesh
Into one, two raindrops
That fall one on top
Of each other
To make one big drop
On the leaf
Of bright
Unending
Winter love.

Transitions

The moonlit glow is
Hovering over horizon's habitat
Churning waters
Restless path oasis
Anchoring from safe harbors
To thundering sanctuary heaven
Cackling rocks
Shimmering, erupting tides
Collide in unleashed caverns

Runaway Trains

We are a runaway train that only subsides
When sharing embracing unites,
And our fiery souls ignite
Into a sigh of
Eden's garden forbidden delight
Radiating our soul's mirror of eternal light
Upon Heaven's gate's site.
There, passion becomes the ultimate flame
Beyond the realm of human pride or shame
We are a runaway train that only subsides
When this kind of sharing and
Ethereal embracing unites,

Angel

As translucent angels,
Winter Solstice melodies
Echo through
Canyon hallways,
Desert oasis
Leaves of golden amber
Reflect its mirrored,
Sculpted magnificence
Over windswept cloud pyramids
Enterlocking, evolving in a transient
Sky-wonderland
In constant motion
Aries spinning
As unleashed emotions triumph
To escalating heights
Lighting up the Universe's
Dark corridors
In a sundrenched awakening
Absorbed like a sponge.
My heart swims in your reservoir
Of Love's marble sanctuary,
Overflowing emotions flood
The Earth's core
Until its presence be known
As the Requiems are reborn
Uniting from the past
Entering the present
As our souls unfold onto a
Spiraling vine spreading
Until we feel its presence
Like tinkling waterfalls
Cleansing our minds and quenching our souls
As spirits unfold into a velvet lace
Of raptured Paradise of unending love
Molded and Chiseled in a deep vastness
Filling the valleys and harvesting our oneness.

In Praise of Women

Women are the real architects of society.

The thing women must do to rise to power is to redefine their femininity. Once power was considered a masculine attribute. In fact, power has no sex.

Anyone who says he can see through women is missing a lot.

"I don't mind living in a man's world as long as I can be a woman in it." That's fair! Women can be pretty in many ways. Their looks change as you get to know them, because you start seeing them from the inside. Their beauty grows on you, depending on their personality and their character.

A woman is like a good suspense movie. The more left to the imagination, the more exciting she is.

A poet looks at the world as a man looks at a woman.

There is in every woman's heart a spark which lies dormant in the times of prosperity, which kindles up and ignites into a fiery blaze in the dark hour of adversity.

Stephen Smoke

Stephen Smoke is the author of 20 novels, including *Black Butterfly*, *Pacific Coast Highway*, *Pacific Blues*, *Trick of the Light*, *The Prince of Palos Verdes*, and *Cathedral of the Senses* under his own and other names. He has also written eight non-fiction books.

Stephen has written and directed feature films, including *Street Crimes* (starring Dennis Farina) and *Final Impact*, and has written screenplays for others, including *Magic Kid*.

In 2011 he published the first novel with its own embedded soundtrack: *Cathedral of the Senses*. The songs on the album (Cathedral of the Senses) were written by Stephen and recorded mainly by musicians and singers living in Sedona. All the songs are available for download via iTunes, Amazon, and other popular music download sites.

In July of 2012 Stephen re-released *Trick of the Light*, which is the prequel to *Cathedral of the Senses*. In 1989 he recorded an album (in support of the *Trick of the Light* novel) on which several well-known musicians, including Rock and Roll Hall of Fame member Garth Hudson (the keyboard player for The Band) played on various tracks. The new edition of *Trick of the Light* was released in softcover and eBook formats, plus an enhanced multimedia version for the iPad. The enhanced edition contains portions of the songs embedded at appropriate points in the novel. The songs are available at all popular music download sites.

The re-release of *Trick of the Light* coincided with the publication of Stephen's novel, *I, Walt Whitman* (in softcover and eBook formats, along with an enhanced multimedia version for the iPad).

With the publication of *Cathedral of the Senses, Trick of the Light,* and *I, Walt Whitman* in all three formats (softcover, eBook, and enhanced multimedia format for the iPad), Stephen has the unique distinction of being a novelist with three multimedia eBooks, each containing its own embedded soundtrack.

Stephen founded and published *Mystery Magazine,* and published the first online mystery magazine (*Hamilton Caine's Mystery Digest*).

He is also a published songwriter. He is a member of ASCAP and regularly collects royalties for music he has written. He occasionally plays at local coffeehouses and other venues.

Stephen is the author of the *Bill of Responsibilities* series and the *Teen Bill of Responsibilities Course,* which is taught in several Southern California schools.

Stephen is an expert in the field of digital publishing. He advises writers and publishers, and specializes in the following: book marketing, eBook conversion, creating enhanced multimedia eBooks, and Indie Publishing in general.

You can contact Stephen through his website: *www.StephenSmoke.com.*

***

I HAVE SEEN THE HEART OF MAN

I have seen the Heart of Man

Red river bleeding dark and deep
Flowing to the sea
Beyond the sea
Beyond what we see

I have seen the Soul of Man
Dim to dark
Flickering in shadows
Struggling to see
Something
Anything
That lasts

The World of Man
Is here and gone
Seasons come
Seasons go
What is born
Shall surely die
All we hold dear
Slips away
Those with whom
We spend our nights
Will be gone
When morning breaks

It is fear that creates the masks we wear
It is fear that we are not the men in our songs
Not the husbands we wish to be
Not the fathers
Not the sons
Not the friends
We wish to be

It is fear that it will all fall away
And all
And nothing
Will be revealed

I have seen darkness shine
Against the Light
Darkness born of fear
Of separation
And so we hide
Put on the show
That becomes a life
Staged by characters
That we are not
Yet wish to be
Or fear to be

Still longing seeps
From deep within
A fatal wound
Bleeding out
To pools of sorrow
Where future drowns
In deep regret

Longing…
To be comfortable where I am
Behind eyes that look upon the world
And wish not
To change
Resist
Or own it

This is peace
To know the world will pass away
To know it all comes and goes
To know that neither flesh nor trouble lasts

To know this and hold it in your heart
Makes precious all you see

Those who know this simple truth:
  Do not try to catch the wind
  But cherish what can't be lost
See no beginning
Nor an end

I have seen the Heart of Man

* * *

(from the novel, *Cathedral of the Senses)*

THE BOOK OF TIME

Ah, the sticky web of time
    Ensnares our moments past
A melancholy theme is heard
    Nothing ever lasts

Memories like just-glimpsed ghosts
    Dance in and out of view
Remind me of another time
    Remind me so of you

When all we had were fragile dreams
    When dreams came out to play
It seems so very long ago
    And yet like yesterday

The Book of Time is infinite
    Its pages cut through years
It holds the smile that's seen no more
    And all forgotten tears

Laughter echoes through silent nights
    Like haunting carols sung
By angels who have gone before
    And wait for us to come

But there's no rush for me to go
    Nor do I try to hide
Someday a door in time will lead
    Me to the other side

The Book of Time is not a work
    That reads well front to end
Uninitiated eyes
    Strain to comprehend

Quicksilver in the mind of God
    Memories are cast
In shapes and sounds that help us sleep
    And make sense of the past

Shadows dance on walls of pain
    To music of the heart
We see the things we want to see
    From which we cannot part

Moments strung like Christmas lights
    That flicker off, then on
The past is past, I see that now
    And yet it's never gone

The liquid lights of yesterday
    Burn like flowing coal
Rivers that connect our minds
    To landscapes of the soul

Such terrain is what it is
    And cannot be explained
Can always be experienced
    But seldom be maintained

Design so vast, infinity
    Can't be contained in years
Obvious in children's eyes
    Alive in old men's tears

Ah, the sticky web of time
    Ensnares our moments past
A joyous, peaceful theme is heard
    When you're here at last

THE DANCE OF DREAMS

Children dance the dance of dreams
  Till from their sleep they wake
Such innocence is precious gold
   Lost when morning breaks

The world is wide and welcoming
  When seen through children's eyes
They see the world as it is
  Before they learn to cry

Through valleys and the darkest nights
  The tears of angels run
To oceans that connect us all
  And make the many one

But such connection's hard to see
  And seldom what it seems
Unseen by most since they were young
  And danced the dance of dreams

DEEP IN THE NOW AND NOW AGAIN

We tend to see
   What we believe
And disregard the rest

When what we see
   Just keeps us safe
Perhaps we miss the best

Such narrow sight
   Makes thieves of men
Who counterfeit their time

And overlook
   The masterpiece
A sad and subtle crime

Baptized in lies
   When I was young
Submerged by my own hand

Yet I am blessed
   To rise again
As Here and Now expand

Yes there are times
   When I can see
What's Now and Now again

And moments clear
   Wash over me
Life tears that seek to mend

THE GRAVITY OF TEARS

For My Buddy, Ace

November 12, 1993 – February 25, 2008

You know I miss you till it aches
I kiss ashes in a jar
I touch the pillow where you slept
And wonder where you are

Because you are so much more
Than flesh and blood and bone
The sacred spark that gave them life
Must have another home

Do you see me as I weep
Do you feel pain I feel
Or are you in a better place
Life's dream no longer real

You'll live forever in my heart
Though broken it will mend
Stitched together with the hope
That true love never ends

Time can be a comfort now
In healing I must do
But seconds seem like years today
Slow motion thoughts of you

When I look into the yard
I see you running there
Strong and brave and beautiful
I say a silent prayer

If I calculate our bond
I can't just count the years
But I can weigh my emptiness
In gravity of tears

We know there is a final act
We'll stand before death's door
Is there a better exit line:
"I could not have loved you more."

MONET AND OTHER FAVORITE PAINTERS

What is more valuable
  Is really hard to say
A child's crayoned work of art
  Or a signed Monet

I cannot place a price on art
  Depends on what I see
I cannot see through others' eyes
  Just what it means to me

I never had the pleasure
  Of meeting Claude Monet
But I remember the little girl
  Who used to run and play

She was good at many things
  Especially climbing trees
Art was not her first love
  I'd like to think it was me

But she outgrew a father's love
  A big wide world to see
I miss her last sweet goodbye
  Yet I know it had to be

At night I sit alone and look
  At paintings that she did
Was her meaning obvious
  Or was it deeply hid

She did tricks with light and dark
  That made me see things new
Things I'd seen a thousand times
  But always looked right through

She opened up a part of me
  A part I didn't know
She made me laugh, she made me cry
  I guess she made me grow

Sometimes I caress paint she brushed
  Touch canvas touched by her
I don't know what I'm supposed to feel
  Sometimes it's just a blur

I find no answers in her work
  Just questions turned to gray
Do colors really fade that fast
  Dead painters cannot say

Vickey Kalambakal

I've been writing since I was 7—wanna see my treatment of *Peter Pan* from the 1960s? My *career* as a writer began in the late 90's when I was a student at UCLA and had to interview people for a history project. The project was so much fun that I stopped and cogitated for a while. My thoughts were simple:

People get paid to do this?

Maybe I could get paid to do this!

And that was it. I finished school with a Masters in history, all with the goal of being a writer. Since I was in my 40s at the time, this held a bit of risk. But my daughter was grown and I had no one to support but myself. I went for it.

I've written for greeting card companies, magazines, textbooks & encyclopedias, online sites like Patch.com, and book series like *Uncle John's Bathroom Reader.*

The first selection here is from my historical novel *Death Speaker.* If you like it, I invite you to read the first few chapters free at DeathSpeaker.com or (better yet!) buy the book.

The second selection showcases mosaics in the South Bay area. I love mosaics; I feature one weekly on my blog, HistoryLosAngeles.blogspot.com. We have beautiful art all around us here. If you haven't noticed them already, pull over for a look the next time you go to the bank, cemetery, or church.

DEATH SPEAKER

(published under the name Vickey Kall)

Emyn never thought before she spoke. Maybe that was why the dead had such an easy time speaking through her.

What were the ghosts saying as she stirred? The words faded, but battles had raged in her sleep. Emyn remembered seas lit with flame; men shrieked as they ran out of the water. There she stood in the middle of it all, unable to look away as waves lapped at her feet.

She heard the dead chattering over the rustle of leaves and muttered, "No one listens to you."

The boy curled beside her, then shifted and rolled his head onto her arm. Emyn didn't move. She had seen too much death in her twenty-three years, but so had Gorio in a lesser span. She let him sleep and soon she dreamed again.

The skull temple burned around her. Roman soldiers trampled and smashed the bones until only a circle of broken skulls remained—a sacred circle that no one could cross.

Was time a line or a circle?

Emyn jerked awake, sure that a real voice had asked the question. Gorio slept on. She stared at the stars, the only side of the world left unchanged. They shone like the year's first snow dusting a field.

Questions raised in dreams had no answers, did they? How could time be a circle? The druids said it was, but they could argue the stars into daylight given the chance.

Time had no end and no beginning, the wise said.

That was silly; everything began somewhere. She'd been born. You philosophers, Emyn told a druid once, you are tricksters who play with words and tell lies that wouldn't fool a child. He tried explaining time to her, but she was stubborn and didn't want to understand.

"Our lives continue in a circle; they don't end."

"But when you make a circle you begin it," Emyn had insisted. "You start somewhere. Don't laugh. . . ."

She could almost hear his deep voice in the darkness. "Rebirth, over and over. We're in this world or the next. We are never nowhere."

The druids were wrong, Emyn decided. There were beginnings and endings, even to time. Her own people were gone and Rome had destroyed the last hope of the Veneti yesterday. Her death was near; she knew that as if she'd caught its scent on the breeze.

The holy places, the secret gods and stories known only to the people of Samarnum—all this existed only in her mind. No one would tell her story when she died; it seemed important to recall it now.

MOSAICS AROUND US

Mosaics are pictures made of bits of stone or tile or glass. They can be primitive: big chunks of porcelain jammed together in cement to form a flower or sun like a child's puzzle; or they can be intricate, each tiny, multifaceted piece perfectly placed to catch the light while adding color and contour to a larger image.

I cannot imagine the patience and experience necessary to design a mosaic. I stand in awe of artists who have not only the skill and artistic vision to create on such a scale, but also the mechanical coordination to build up the picture.

You've no doubt seen mosaic floors at the Getty Villa or in textbooks. Romans loved mosaics, and so did the Byzantines—those later Romans who lived in what is now Istanbul. Would you be surprised to know that the South Bay is full of mosaics as well? Some are by famous artists; many are unsigned.

I don't do poetry. But I figure that writing about mosaics—especially if I can throw in some photos—is about as close to true artistry as mortals can get.

Millard Sheets and Home Savings and Loan

Baby boomers like me remember the Home Savings and Loan banks with their murals, mosaics, and stained glass windows. Howard Ahmanson built that chain of banks starting in the 1950s, and wanted them to be different and beautiful. So he called on Millard Sheets.

Sheets was a well-known artist and teacher long before he started designing banks for Howard Ahmanson, but he'd never dabbled in architecture. Yet that's what Ahmanson wanted him to do: design banks and fill them with original artwork. Ahmanson was bored with the look of the buildings he saw. He wanted something different and told Sheets he had carte blanche to decide what "something different" would be.

In fact, when Sheets called Ahmanson to make sure the boss was ok with the amount of money Sheets was spending on the first bank, Ahmanson hung up on him! The financier was quite serious. The design was in Sheets' hands.

Fortunately, Ahmanson had chosen well. The two men worked together for decades, although the relationship could be volatile. In all, Sheets designed or approved more than 40 buildings and decorated them with paintings, mosaics, stained glass, and sculpture.

One of those buildings is on the Palos Verdes Peninsula.

A Home Savings and Loan went up near the corner of Hawthorne and Silver Spur in 1974, and the facade is covered with mosaic images from our Ranchero days: men and women on horseback, followed by playful dogs, all set against the disk of the sun on the horizon and framed in black marble.

Washington Mutual took over most Home S&Ls in 1999, including that Rolling Hills branch on Hawthorne. After 30 years, the salty air from the sea was corroding the mortar that held the mosaic together. As the bank's owner, WaMu agreed to repair the 37-foot wide mosaic, but when the economy tanked in 2008, Chase Bank took over the chain. No one knew what would happen next.

Thankfully, Chase Bank came through with a $400,000 restoration, and today the mosaic is as beautiful as ever.

There are other places with mosaics in the South Bay that started out as Home Savings and Loan: A Chase Bank and the Time Warner offices in Torrance, for example. But one building in Redondo Beach—at Torrance Blvd and PCH—was never intended to be permanent. It still stands, though.

By 1979, Howard Ahmanson had died and Millard Sheets was retired. Home S&L erected a prefabricated building next to the Cozy Cafe, just blocks from the beach. Even though the tiny Cozy Cafe had been there since the 1940s, the banking firm apparently thought they could buy the property and get rid of the Cafe.

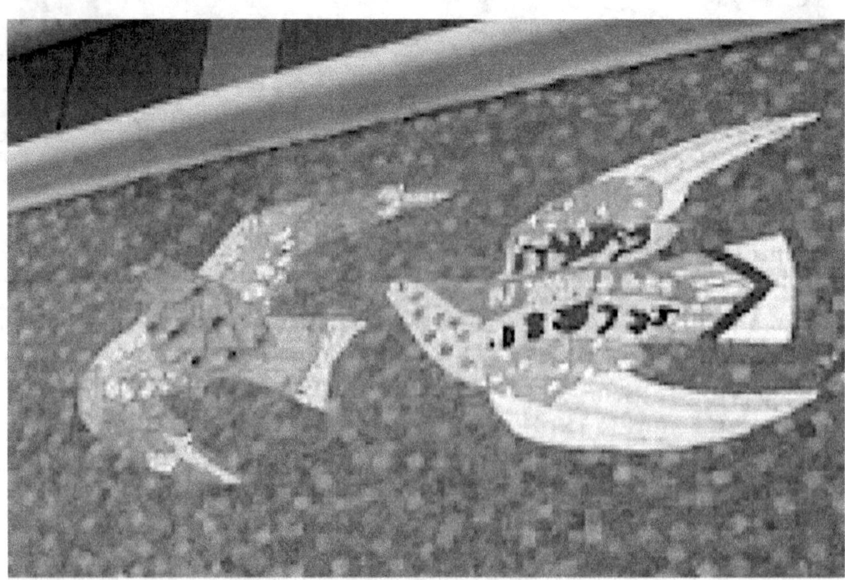

They were so sure that they could build a big new bank on the corner that they had Susan Hertel—who was running Millard Sheets' design firm—make two beautiful mosaics featuring birds in flight, one for each entrance of the proposed building.

Flash forward to 2011. The Cozy Cafe is still serving up eggs and sausage, but Home Savings and Loan is long gone. A Wells Fargo Bank operates out of that prefab building. One mosaic, facing Torrance Blvd, is losing tiles. The other has been completely forgotten because it faces the back of the Cozy Cafe.

Although I didn't know the mosaic's history at the time, I was sad to see it deteriorate. I asked an editor at Patch.com, an online news service, if I could write a story about it. She gave me the go-ahead and I called Wells Fargo's corporate headquarters. Eventually I got hold of people who cared passionately about their company's history. They were thrilled to hear about the mosaic and promised to restore it. A few weeks later, art conservators discovered the second mosaic when they set up their scaffolding.

That both artworks were restored—even though one is still hidden—made me very proud. I learned that a writer doesn't need to catch a politician doing something naughty in order to exert her influence.

More Mosaics

At Peck Park in San Pedro, girl scouts, families, moms from the Art to Grow On group, and students from local schools all helped artist Julie Bender shape and fire tiles, set them, and create a huge new mosaic that faces the swimming pool. That happened over the first half of 2012, when city budgets were being slashed to the bone. I find it amazing that such a project could take place and turn out so beautifully, but the South Bay is not only home to talented artists, but to people who love and appreciate art. When they work together, miracles take place.

You can see one panel of that Peck Park mosaic at the end of this article.

Volunteers assembled the mosaic steps leading from the International Boardwalk to the Village Condos in Redondo Beach, shown on the previous page. Look for them next time you're in the area. Two employees of Tulita Elementary School—Debbie Collette and Patti Linett—organized the effort and created the original artwork.

The same artists designed mosaics on several bollards (short pillars) along the Esplanade—the first in a series of mosaics that are unfunded and donated by the artists and their helpers. Why? To beautify Redondo Beach.

On Lomita Blvd east of Narbonne, look for the Summer Studio Arts Academy. Outside its doors is a mosaic representing the city of Lomita. It was put up in 2009 with the help of over 50 people who just wanted to be part of the project. It's pictured at the start of this article.

Green Hills Memorial Park in Rancho Palos Verdes has installed several mosaics to honor veterans at a World War II Memorial on its grounds, depicting sscenes of the Harbor area. They also display floral mosaics along the outer walls of its vaults.

I haven't mentioned churches, libraries, or schools, have I? Well, they're full of mosaics too—even on the outside. Some eye-catching exterior mosaics include those on St. Lawrence Martyr Catholic Church on Prospect in Redondo Beach, Our Lady of Guadalupe in Hermosa Beach, Mary Star of the Sea in San Pedro, the North Torrance Library on Artesia, the Mayme Dear Library in Gardena, and at least a dozen schools in San Pedro and the Palos Verdes communities. Some of these were done in the 1960s, others just yesterday. Some were executed by famed mosaicists, other by groups of unpaid helpers following the direction of an artist volunteering his or her time.

In fact, once you start paying attention, you will find mosaics all over. And finding beauty all over is Good. Some might even say it's the point of art and of life itself.

***

The mosaic mermaid at Peck Park in San Pedro, CA.

William Whittenbury

William Whittenbury began writing as soon as he could, and never stopped. He writes in many genres, but is especially proud of his contributions for this anthology. “Showdown” was inspired by William’s experiences in elementary school. On the playground, groups of children would form “countries,” and the playground became a complex web of political intrigue. Sometimes, these countries would go to war with each other, and “Showdown” describes one of these conflicts through the eyes of the children.

“The Cathedral of Democracy” was inspired by William’s great love for both skyscrapers and the Art Deco movement of the 1920s and 1930s. The poem, which refers to the Empire State Building, was inspired by Emma Lazarus’ epic sonnet “The New Colossus.”

“Unfallen” was written spur-of-the moment to commemorate the tenth anniversary of the 9/11 terrorist attacks on New York City. He hopes that the message about the Freedom Tower at the end of the piece will inspire readers to believe that we can do anything, no matter what knocks us down.

SHOWDOWN

The day had come. The drums sounded. The red flag fluttered over the ramparts. Gunners ran out the cannons. Blacksmiths hammered weapons out of solid ingots of iron. This was the day. This was the day.

Our nation's precipitous decline had hit rock bottom. We were once the most powerful in the world. Our quartered flag once flew from the forests of Nest all the way to the burning asphalt desert of Bornquini. Our patrols once scoured the Muskwan Mountains, protecting the natural resources and resolving disputes. Our engineering was unparalleled. Our supremacy was unassailable. Even the fierce Hawks to the West or the Lunytopians to the north couldn't match us.

Until he came.

Josiah used to be the finest citizen in the Republic. As the Scout Master, he led our Muskwan scout corps to a successful outcome time after time. Then, he broke a law. We had no choice but to banish him. Flung from the gates of the capital, Zenna, he stumbled about the northern plains as he burned with rage. Revenge was his only thought; his insides turned whenever he saw that red, quartered flag of ours. Then, vengeance struck.

From the plains of the north rose a terrifying new nation. Sweeping before him all those who felt oppressed by us or our allies, he built the largest army the world had ever seen. A few of the tribes he seduced, the Murundigans, rebelled and joined us. The rest turned to Josiah as the savior. Our provinces of Nest and Ruger fell with almost no resistance. We begged the Hawks and Lunytopians for help, but even they were afraid, instead migrating away from Josiah's armies to safer grounds. Our troops turned and ran whenever Josiah's avenging army was sighted.

Until today.

Josiah had crossed the line. He had advanced too far. Now, he would hear the roar of Muskwan guns.

Josiah had created a cult of personality with his people, so much so that his subjects worshipped him. His country was nothing short of fascist, and it ruled half the world. But he didn't rule Zenna.

The City of Zenna was built high in the hills where the Muskwan Mountains bend to the west, surrounding a gigantic tree. Nobody knows how old the tree is, but it provides a great comfort to our people. Zenna had once been the glorious center of the civilized world. Now, it was a grim, besieged fortress. Its shining walls are stained with gunpowder. But our quartered flag still fluttered defiantly in the chill breeze. We resolved that we would never surrender.

The leaves of the Zenna tree rustled in the breeze as a small bee journeyed from flower to flower. Beneath our feet, a gopher dug a new tunnel system. A hawk wheeled overhead, its tail sending great red rays of sunlight over the land. A sparrow zipped about. The oats bent to the wind, their seed pods scattering with the dandelions that rode the updrafts as expertly as any bird. All was still as we waited, clutching our muskets. All was still.

The cry of the lookout cracked through the air like a bullet as he screamed from his high tower, "Here they come!"

We hefted our rifles and raced down the stone road to the plain. There, we took position in a defense trench along with our war horses, waiting for the horde that we knew was coming.

We watched as a huge dust cloud billowed into the sky, the motes sparkling in the sunlight. The thunder of hooves and running feet reached our ears as the ground shook. Then, a terrifying sound assaulted our ears as Josiah's men uttered their war cry.

We weren't afraid. We were finished cowering behind Zenna's walls. Uttering our own war cry, we rose as one and fired our guns with a deafening crackle. The cannons on the walls roared. Huge plumes of dirt clouded the sky as our shells hit home. Deafening explosions shook us to the core as blinding flashes seared our eyes. My heart gave a small jump as I looked up and saw our magnificent flag snapping in the wind. A lump formed in my throat as I wondered if this was the last day that banner would ever wave.

Josiah's men were taken aback by our defiance. Shifty-eyed and nervous, they peered about them as their steps faltered. With panicked expressions, they began to herd themselves backward, flinching before our fire.

Before they became Josiah's slaves, these men were humble nomadic tribesmen from the north. They bickered among themselves, and would never stand as one. If they formed ranks, they would break and run at the first sign of enemy aggression. Now, they were a precision-trained force urged on by Josiah's high, raspy voice, but a grain of fear for us still ran deep in all of them. A few began to break and run.

"FORWARD, FORWARD, COWARDS! FIGHT FOR THE GLORY OF OUR NATION! CRUSH THE OPPRESSOR! MAKE THEM PAY! BE BOLD! BE STRONG!" The high, raspy voice rang out above the din of battle. I watched adoration flash before the eyes of the enemy, and a new fire burned in their eyes as the retreat was reversed. With the rat-a-tat of their muskets behind them, the enemy charged.

The host approached rapidly, covering ground at an alarming rate. Some of our gunfire began to falter, as our troops realized we were outnumbered and overmatched. Bullets rained down on us in great hails of fury. We ducked anew every time the enemy fired a volley. To charge from the trench would be suicide. Our fire tapered off until only a few sporadic bursts resisted the enemy army. Now, only Zenna's guns were keeping the enemy from completely surrounding our trench. We would all surely die if help did not arrive, and no help would come. We had no allies besides the few Murundigans that had joined us. Muskwa stood alone against the greatest evil the world had ever seen, and we had failed.

Then, something hit Josiah's flank like a thunderbolt. All at once, his lines collapsed. His troops lost all order, their eyes rolling in panic. Something had changed.

A high-pitched screech reminiscent of the cry of a raptor split the air, assaulting our ears. Josiah's men parted like the red sea, their eyes like those of horses faced with a fire.

From our trench, we caught a magnificent sight. A horse stood proud upon a high rock outcropping, its rider screeching like a bird. Her green robes billowed about her like the avenging wings of a raptor. The Hawks had arrived.

The Hawks were fierce horsewomen from the southern steppes. They lived a nomadic lifestyle, and fiercely resisted intruders. They took no prisoners. Nobody who ventured into their territory ever came back. We had an uneasy peace with them, which mostly revolved around trade of their natural resources for our manufactured goods. The Hawks had not officially declared war against Josiah, but they were unnerved by him. Now, they had come to save us. Why, we weren't sure.

More gunfire erupted from the west. The armies of Lunytopu, another friendly nation to the northwest, had come to save us as well! The Republic would endure!

As Josiah's army fled before the new onslaught, we mounted our war-horses that were in the trench, spurring them forward as we screamed our battle cry, "MAVERNMORN!" Thundering forward, we smashed into the retreating enemy, hurling our mud grenades in all directions. Muskwa's decline would be avenged.

Within Josiah's ranks, chaos reigned. His troops milled about, dropping their weapons and panicking. Soldier after soldier threw up his arms and surrendered. The Hawks cut a wide swath through the roiling mass of bodies, forging a path directly towards Josiah. As his guards deserted him, he found himself face-to-face with Theodora, the Hawk's fiercest warrior.

A despondent cry split the air as Josiah fell.

Unharmed but humiliated, he began to crawl hand-over-hand towards open ground and safety. Shock covered the faces of his dumbstruck men. Then, one enemy soldier started to laugh. Then another. And another. Soon, Josiah's entire host threw down their weapons as they realized that their fearful leader wasn't invincible after all. His promises were empty. He was powerless. He ruled by fear, and that fear was gone. As their awe perished, so did the evil within them. Laughing, they raced across the battlefield to embrace their Murundigan brothers in our army.

The sun broke from behind a cloud, filling the field with radiant, joyous light. The rays sparkled in the dewdrops that laced themselves among the grass. The great nations of the world were one. Together, we had vanquished evil and learned to forgive.

Even Josiah was forgiven. As he crawled away, myself and two others bore him up, letting him stand again. With a grateful look in his eye, he jumped on a horse and rode to the east, never to be seen on the field again.

From deep within our hearts, we thanked our friends from Hawkland and Lunytopu for saving our nation. Why, I asked, had they bothered to help us? "That's what friends are for," Theodora replied with a smile on her face and a twinkle in her eye. As the smoke cleared from the battlefield, all eyes turned to the Muskwan flag fluttering beside the great tree in the city of Zenna. We had won.

A great peal of a bell rang through the air, and, laughing as friends, we ran to the west.

As the fourth-graders returned to their classroom from recess, the leaves of a tree high on a slope in the playground whispered in the breeze.

THE CATHEDRAL OF DEMOCRACY

Towering above Earth's greatest city
Sprung from the glory of a land born free
That pillar of steel, that symbol of pride
Bathed in the light of the sun that it scrapes
Tumbling like a cascade at each setback
Its spire gleaming, reaching yet higher
Hefting its lofty winged head o'er all
To the tyrants to the ancient world
It screams the defiance of the people
The power of the new land of freedom
Crowned with bright light stemming from liberty
The streets about it bask in the glow of
The new Cathedral of Democracy!

UNFALLEN:
IN MEMORY OF THE TWIN TOWERS

Far greater than the Doric, Ionic, or Corinthian
In their surpassing glory
Shooting straight skyward, two columns that surpass
The grandeur of a pagan Olympus
Audacious and daring in their forthright, proud faces
Slab-sided, standing tall in defiance of the roiling sea
Flanking the sea-washed Mother of Exiles, they silently cry
"We are of the greatest nation on Earth, the republic of Freedom!
The New World, vast in its strength,
Built on the resolve of the free!"

They complement the defiant decree of the symbol of liberty
As they rise a quarter of a mile into the sky
What shall bring their hoary heads down from their lofty height?
Two planes, Chained to the will of a religion-crazed maniac
Pulled from their noble duty to commit an act of death
Flying to destroy the cause of freedom
Bearing the lives of those confused and enslaved
Slam into those proud towers

In the eyes of the evil, as they burn
They see the death of freedom
As the towers crumble and fall
They see us humiliated in defeat

They are wrong.

Out of the sky dark with ash
Out of the rubble filled with sorrow
The glory dragged back down to Earth
The anguish of a grieving city

Arises a new nation
United in resolve and defiant spirit
Fifty states working together,
Spread in great glory across the face of a continent
Forged into the hardest steel from the flames of that fire

From the place where they once stood arises a new song
Like a phoenix from the flame
For we are proud to be American
And we are unbroken
From the rubble of dreams thought by evil to be extinguished
Arise two beams of light, high into the heavens

Now those twin towers symbolize much more
The goal of their destruction has been futile
They symbolize not finance or wealth of a pompous nation
They symbolize the steely resolve
Of a people united by their freedom
To us they still stand tall
For they will always live on in our hearts
Though they have ascended in all their glory
Finally surmounting the heavens that they tried their best to scale

As the new column, resplendent in its glory,
Rises above the greatest city on Earth,
We remember those who died on that awful day
And rejoice in the new tower, brimming with its clear message.
With its own silent voice it cries,

"Thou art futile, devils of evil! For you attempts to break us have been in vain. In smiting us so we fall down, you have caused us to rise higher! For Liberty can never be broken, for freedom can never be extinguished! For right will always win and evil shall never prevail! See, ye people of the Earth, this testament to the resolve of the American people! My Spire soars ever high above the golden door!"

OUR HISTORY

THE HISTORY OF THE SOUTHWEST MANUSCRIPTERS ... SO FAR.

by Edith Battles and Ian Gordon

"**Southwest Manuscripters** was the bright offspring of the fading **Los Angeles Manuscripters** born early in the 20th Century (it had been around since the late 1930's). In the fall of 1949, Hermosans **Ramoncita O'Connor**, **Zella Allison**, **Kay Snow** and **Walt Darby** founded the new group whose combined years make it the longest-active writers organization west of the Rockies. I came aboard a month later, in time to hear the fabulous first speaker, **Ray Bradbury**, tell of his newly minted ***Martian Chronicles***."

Ray Bradbury

So wrote charter member Edith Battles in her ***"Half a Century with Southwest Manuscripters"***, a historical essay written especially for the club.

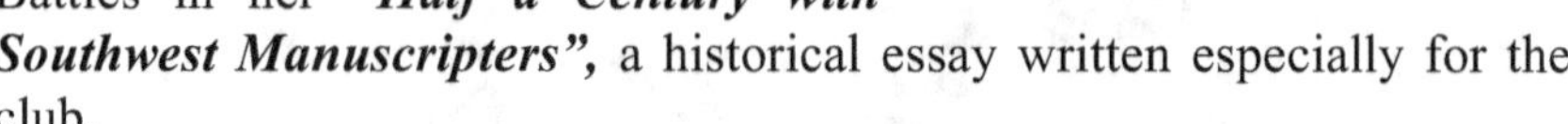

She continues by saying that, "**Mona O'Connor**, the first president, was no feminist; she bowed hastily to the group vote for **Sam Stewart**, balladeer and editor of ***The Daily Breeze***, and succeeding male presidents including science fiction writers **Mark Clifton**, **Raymond Banks** and **Maurice Ogden**. Men prevailed during those early years while women rounded up the speakers and cookies and coffee each meeting."

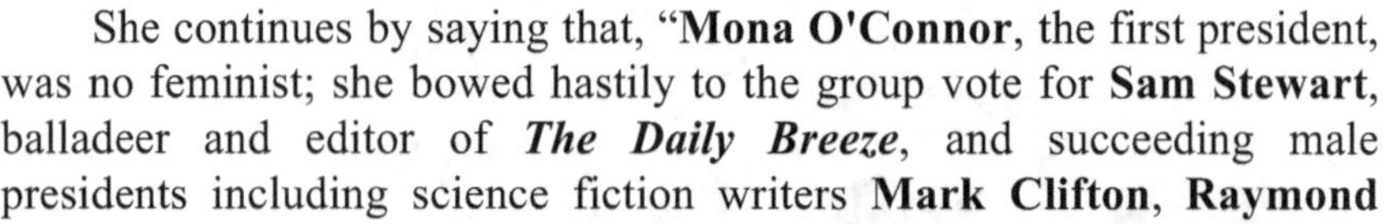

Clark Stadium in a frequently fog-filled valley in **Hermosa Beach** was the meeting place for several decades. This was followed by locations such as the **Pacific Inn** in Torrance and the recent **Palos Verdes Peninsula Library**.

Ray Bradbury

"While never spending a penny," Edith says, "**Southwest Manuscripters** induced top-notch writers to come and talk. **Rod Serling**,

Adela Rogers St. John, **Frank Riley**, **Hannibal Coons** and many other popular fiction and non-fiction writers came. Before the Love Boat was launched into its two-generation career, **The Manuscripters** presented the author **Linda Bloodworth**, of later TV and Clinton fame, told members of her first break as a screenwriter.

And every year we could snag him, **Ray Bradbury** came back."

As this history proceeds, I intend to expand on these stories of our guest speakers, but the real story was that of our members, who went on to their own fame as writers.

As she goes on, Edith explains, "Careers began and were helped along in **Manuscripters**. When first class postage was just three cents, many of us, inspired by the monthly sales reports of fellow members, submitted our early efforts and gained a foothold. **Jimmie Butler** presided while he wrote best-selling hi-tech novels. **Dave Kenny** wrote humor and whimsy while wielding the gavel. When the ladies finally left the kitchen for the presidency, **Wanda Smith, Rustie Brown** and **Ellen Doukoulas** were all productive writers. My own sales were scattered shots through magazine-dom, but I got my book momentum through my membership. The **Southwest Manuscripters** was the seed for local writing courses long before college extension courses made such study available."

Edith Battles was too modest, she went on to write many poems, articles and well-read children's books, many of which are still in print today.

Ray Bradbury & Edith Battles

Ramoncita "Mona" O'Connor was our founding President and helped to organize most of the structure of our group. She has sold in virtually all mediums of writing. Her poetry has appeared in the Saturday Evening Post and Wall street Journal.

Here is one of her poems, which was published in several newspapers and magazines:

DISILLUSION

"My dreams were all of caravans
And gaily costumed throngs,
Black horses shod with silver shoes
and haunting gypsy songs.

Today, I saw a gypsy van come
struggling to the rise,
I turned my head lest they should see
The tears leap to my eyes.

– **Ramoncita S. O'Connor**

Her juvenile stories have appeared in many children's magazines. She has also published articles and books. ***"Murder Won't Wait,"*** one of her mysteries, may be found in most libraries. **Mrs. O'Connor**, who was a member of the **Southern California Woman's Press Club**, also had classes in creative writing under Adult Education, at Mira Costa High School and a day class at Redondo High School.

She was also a multi-winner of the various club writing contests, besides doing her duty as a judge in those contests.

Ramoncita relinquished her Presidency in 1950 or 1951 to **Kay L. Snow**,

In April of 1953, **Mark Clifton**, who was a Redondo resident, came to speak at the club.

Mark Clifton

Mark Clifton was a science fiction writer who had a very strong connection with ***Astounding Science Fiction's*** long-time editor **John Campbell**. Many of his short stories, which were written in collaboration with **Alex Apostolides** or **Frank Riley** were published in that renown magazine. He later went on to get several of his longer stories published in book form, also with **Frank Rhylich**, or **Frank Riley** as was his pseudonym.

Mark Clifton returned at least six times as a speaker and became club President in 1957 and again in 1963.

Pierre Boesch was the club **President** in 1953 and the **Manuscripters** hosted **Adela Rogers St. Johns** in January, **Louis L'Amour** in March, **Mark Clifton** in April, **Jack Webb** in May... and in August of 1953, the notorious **Leonard Wibberley**. Quite an impressive line-up!

Adela Rogers St. Johns was an American journalist, novelist, actress and screenwriter best known as a reporter for Hearst newspapers and for her interviews of motion picture stars.

Adela Rogers St. Johns

The daughter of a noted criminal lawyer, **St. Johns** often went to courtrooms in her youth. She began her career in journalism, as well as her long association with **Hearst Publications**, in 1913 as a reporter for the **San Francisco Examiner**, and she subsequently worked for **William Randolph Hearst's Los Angeles Herald**, **Chicago American**, **New York American**, and **International News Service**. She reported on crime, politics, society, and sports news before retiring in the early 1920s. **St. Johns** then became noted for interviewing movie stars for **Photoplay** magazine. She also wrote short stories for **Cosmopolitan**, the **Saturday Evening Post,** and other magazines, finishing 9 of her 13 screenplays before returning to reporting for **Hearst** newspapers.

Writing in a distinctive, emotional style, **St. Johns** reported on, among other subjects, the controversial **Jack Dempsey-Gene Tunney** "long-count" fight in 1927, the treatment of the poor during the **Great Depression**, and the 1935 trial of **Richard Bruno Hauptmann** for kidnapping and murdering the son of **Charles Lindbergh**. In the mid-1930s she moved to Washington, D.C., to report on national politics. Her coverage of the assassination of **Senator Huey Long** in 1935, the abdication of **King Edward VIII** of Britain in 1936, the **Democratic National Convention** of 1940, and other major stories made her one of the best-known reporters of the day. She said in her autobiography, ***The Honeycomb*** (1969), that what she did not learn at school she had "learned from pimps, professional prostitutes, gamblers, bank robbers, poets, newspapermen, jury bribers, millionaire dipsomaniacs, and murderers."

St. Johns retired again from newspaper work in 1948 in order to write books, including novels and memoirs, and to teach at a series of universities. In 1970 she was awarded the **Medal of Freedom**. In 1976, at the age of 82, she returned to reporting for the **San Francisco Examiner** to cover the bank robbery and conspiracy trial of **Patricia**

Hearst, granddaughter of her former employer.

Louis Dearborn L'Amour was an American author. His books consisted primarily of Western fiction novels, however he also wrote historical fiction, science fiction, nonfiction, as well as poetry and short-story collections. Many of his stories were made into movies. **L'Amour's** books remain popular and most have gone through multiple printings.

Louis L'Amour

At the time of his death most of his 105 existing works were in print and he was considered ***"one of the world's most popular writers"***. **L'Amour** eventually wrote 89 novels, over 250 short stories, and sold more than 320 million copies of his work. By the 1970s his writings were translated into over 20 languages. Every one of his works is still in print.

Mark Clifton was a two-time President of **Southwest Manuscripters** and prolific science fiction author, working with Frank Riley in many of his works. He was a long term member of the club and spoke in front of its membership many times.

Jack Webb really needs no introduction, he will be remembered most for his physically rigid portrayal of the morally rigid cop **Joe Friday** on ***Dragnet***, but he had one of the most varied and far-reaching careers in television history. In his four decades in broadcasting, **Webb** performed nearly every role imaginable in the industry: actor, director, producer, writer (under the pseudonym **John Randolph**), editor, owner of an independent production company, and major studio executive. **Webb's** importance stems not only from his endurance and versatility, but also from his innovation and success.

Jack Webb

After leading roles in radio dramas, **Webb** conceived of his own police program based on discussions with Los Angeles police officers about the unrealistic nature of most "cop" shows. **Dragnet** began on NBC radio in 1949, based on "actual cases" from the files of the L.A.P.D. and featuring **Webb** as director, producer, co-writer, and star in the role of the stoic **Sergeant Joe Friday.**

Dragnet was a huge success, moving to television in 1951 where it became the highest-rated crime drama in broadcast history. The show's success fueled Webb's career as an independent producer and director of both television and feature films. **Webb's Mark VII Limited** production company produced **Dragnet** throughout its run on television. He also produced numerous other shows, including **Adam-12**, **Emergency**, and **General Electric True**. **Webb** directed and produced more feature films throughout the 1950s, most notably an acclaimed version of ***Pete Kelly's Blues*** in 1955.

Dublin-born **Leonard Patrick O'Connor Wibberley**, educated in Ireland and England, abandoned his education in the 1930's to become a reporter in **London**. He spent some time in Trinidad before serving in WWII, and moved to the United States in 1943, doing journalism in **New York** and **Chicago** before finally settling in **California.**

Leonard Wibberley

Although **Leonard Wibberley** is best known for writing ***"The Mouse That Roared,"*** a satire about the tiny **European Duchy of Grand Fenwick** that declares war on the **United States**. He also authored scores of other books in his lifetime. His prolific work spanned many genres, including **historical fiction, science fiction, humor, non-fiction** and **books for children.**

Wibberley also wrote the ***Father Joseph Bredder*** mystery series, about the **Los Angeles** Franciscan priest detective, which are short, fast-moving and full of action.

He was a local, living in **Manhattan Beach** and came back as guest speaker in 1955, 1956 and 1959.

In July of 1953 The **Southwest Manuscripters** were invited to attend a literary tea and garden party hosted by the **Santa Monica Writers Club**.

Maurice Ogden became President for 1954 and **Ray Bradbury** returned for his first public appearance after his recent trip to **Great Britain** where he was assigned the job of scripting the immortal ***Moby Dick*** for motion pictures by **John Huston**.

Maurice Ogden was a known author in his own right, having been a poet, author and lyricist ... His first job in New York was as a writer of the streetcar card ads. He sold a short story to **Street & Smith's Astounding Science Fiction** magazine called ***"Mister Pinshur"*** written in collaboration with club **Secretary Betty Fuller**.

Ogden's most famous piece was a poem called ***"The Hangman"*** which was made into a film narrated by **Herschel Bernardi**, famous for his roles on ***"Peter Gunn"*** on TV and ***"Fiddler on the Roof"*** on stage.

During his tenure as **President**, the **Manuscripters** hosted **Mrs Margaret Leighton**, **Henry Kuttner** and his co-author wife, **C.L. Moore**, **Ray Bradbury** (again), **Hannibal Coons**, **Jack Webb** (again) and **Forrest J. Ackerman**, editor, publisher and authors' agent.

Margaret Leighton was either the famous actress or a well-known author... or both. I have not yet been able to determine which. That is what an ongoing History Project for the club is all about.

Henry Kuttner and **C.L. Moore** were a husband-wife team of authors who wrote mostly science fiction under various pseudonyms, famously, **Lewis Padgett**. He (or they) have been credited by many science fictions authors, including **Ray Bradbury**, as being the best of the classic period of science fiction and a great influence and inspiration for most, if not all.

Henry Kuttner & C.L. Moore

Henry Kuttner was born in **Los Angeles**, California in 1915. His father, the bookseller **Henry Kuttner**, had come from **Prussia** and lived in **San Francisco** since 1859. **Henry Kuttner's** great-grandfather was the scholar, **Josua Heschel Kuttner**. As a young man he worked for the literary agency of his uncle, **Laurence D'Orsay**, in Los Angeles before selling his first story, ***"The Graveyard Rats,"*** to ***Weird Tales*** in early 1936.

Kuttner was known for his literary prose and worked in close collaboration with his wife, **C. L. Moore**. They met through their association with the **"Lovecraft Circle,"** a group of writers and fans who corresponded with **H. P. Lovecraft**. Their work together spanned the 1940s and 1950s and most of the work was credited to pseudonyms, mainly **Lewis Padgett** and **Lawrence O'Donnell.**

Catherine Lucille Moore was an American science fiction and fantasy writer. As **C. L. Moore** she was one of the first women to write in the genre, and paved the way for many other female writers in speculative fiction.

L. Sprague de Camp, who knew **Kuttner** and **Moore** well, has stated that their collaboration was so intensive that, after a story was completed, it was often impossible for either of them to recall who had written which portions.

Marion Zimmer Bradley is among many authors who have cited **Kuttner** as an influence.

Ray Bradbury dedicated ***"Dark Carnival,"*** his first book, to him, calling him one of his hardest-working and most patient teachers. **Bradbury** has said that **Kuttner** actually wrote the last 300 words of **Bradbury's** first horror story, ***"The Candle."*** **Bradbury** has referred to **Kuttner** as a neglected master and a ***"pomegranate writer, popping with seeds - full of ideas."***

In 1945, **Kuttner** and **Moore** wrote the story ***"What You Need,"*** which was adapted into a fine, albeit darker, installment of ***"Tales of Tomorrow"*** and, later, ***"The Twilight Zone."*** Their collaboration spawned hundreds of books, short stories, television and movie scripts. In 2007, **New Line Cinema** released a feature film loosely based on the **Lewis Padgett** short story ***"Mimsy Were the Borogoves"*** under the title ***"The Last Mimzy."***

Hannibal Coons, was born **Stanley J. Coons** the Brother of the American author **Maurice Coons**. They were sons of a theatrical impresario who managed the road tours of the New Orleans Opera Company in **Missouri** in 1909. **Hannibal** was a TV writer for such shows as, ***My Three Sons, Family Affair, The Addams Family, Vacation Playhouse, Petticoat Junction, Bachelor Father,*** and ***Dennis the Menace.***

Forrest J Ackerman was an American collector of science fiction books and movie memorabilia and a science fiction fan. He was, for over seven decades, one of science fiction's staunchest spokesmen and promoters. He was also a magazine

Forrest J Ackerman

editor, science fiction writer and literary agent, a founder of science fiction fandom and the editor and principal writer of the American magazine ***Famous Monsters of Filmland,*** as well as an actor and producer.

He knew most of the writers of science fiction in the first half of the twentieth-century. As a literary agent, he represented some 200 writers, and he served as agent of record for many long lost authors, thereby allowing their work to be reprinted in anthologies. He was **Ed Wood's** "illiterary" agent. He was credited with nurturing and even inspiring the careers of several early contemporaries like **Ray Bradbury**, **Ray Harryhausen**, **Charles Beaumont**, **Marion Zimmer Bradley** and **L. Ron Hubbard**.

Peter Boesch became President again in 1955 and **Ray Bradbury** made his fourth annual visit to the **Southwest Manuscripters**.

That year (1955) also saw guest speakers **Patrice Monahan**, **Associate Editor of Westways Magazine, Robert Stephens**, a fiction writer for **Post** magazine, **Leonard Wibberly** again, **Jay Ransom, Ray E. Banks**, writer and future club **President**, **Mark Clifton** (again) and **Frank Priest,** TV writer.

Mark Clifton came in as **President** in 1956, bringing with him **Beth Norman, Jack Webb, Bert Mitchell Anderson, Harriet Pratt, Leonard Wibberley, Edward J. Ruppelt, Ray Bradbury, Adele Comandini, Nancy Williams, David Duncan** and **Adela Rogers St. Johns** as guest speakers.

Of these not already described, **Edward J. Ruppelt** is perhaps the most interesting. Having been in the **Army Air Corps** during **World War II**, he was released into the Army reserves. Attending **Iowa State College**, he earned an aeronautical engineering degree. Shortly after finishing his education, **Ruppelt** was called back to active military duties after the **Korean War** began.

Capt. Edward J. Ruppelt

He was assigned to the **Air Technical Intelligence Center** headquartered at **Wright-Patterson Air Force Base**. The base had also headquartered two formal **unidentified flying object** investigations: ***"Project Sign"*** and ***"Project Grudge."*** He soon became involved with

"Project Blue Book," a formal governmental study of **unidentified flying objects**. He is generally credited with coining the term ***"unidentified flying object,"*** to replace the misleading terms ***"flying saucer"*** and ***"flying disk."***

He remained with ***Blue Book*** until late 1953. Most observers of ***Blue Book*** agree that the **Ruppelt** years comprised the project's golden age, when investigations were most capably directed and conducted.

In 1956 he worked as a research engineer for **Northrop Aircraft Company**, and wrote his 1956 book ***"The Report on Unidentified Flying Objects."*** The book is notable because it was, for decades, the only account of **Air Force UFO** studies written by a participant.

Douglas Kiefer was **President** in 1957. **Virginia Cox Smith, Frank Ryhlick, Joe Brennan, Maxine Shore, Arthur Julian, Mark Clifton, Harold Braham, Mona O'Connor, W. David Sievers, J.E. Ransom, Maldon Bishop and Ray Bradbury** were the guest speakers that year.

Ray Banks was elected President of **Southwest Manuscripters** in 1958 and **Paul I. Wellman**, noted novelist and historian, President of the **Authors' Club of Los Angeles**, a fellow of the **Society of American Historians**, and a member of the **Academy of Motion Picture Arts and Sciences** was our guest speaker in May.

Edith Battles, Mike Dolinsky, Edith Blackburn, Chas. Beaumont, Paul Wellman, Bert Mitchell Anderson, Ila Limerick, Dorothy Haskin, Ray Bradbury, Dorothy B. Hughes and **Rod Serling** rounded out the remainder of the year.

In February, 1958 we had **Mike "Meyer" Dolinsky**, Los Angeles writer for television, motion pictures and radio, and teacher as a guest speaker. **Dolinsky** was a prolific writer for television, motion pictures.and radio and was a teacher of English and writing at Westchester High School.

Dolinsky's talk featured writing for films and television. His credits included manuscripts for television's ***"Science Fiction Theater," "Matinee Theater," "Dr. Hudson's Secret Journal"*** and ***"Hallmark Hall of Fame."***

He had been completing a Paramount film, and was the author of ***"Hotrod Rumble,"*** both a motion picture and paperback book. He had also written 20 scripts for radio's ***"The Whistler"*** and several for the ***"Escape"*** series.

Charles Beaumont was born in Chicago as **Charles Leroy Nutt.** He sold his first story to ***Amazing Stories*** in 1950. His next big break came when Esquire rejected a science-fiction short story called "The Crooked Man" that depicted a world where heterosexuals were in the minority. In 1955, **Hugh Hefner** agreed to publish it in **Playboy**..

Charles Beaumont

A **"Southern California"** group was loosely formed back then, and among the members were **Richard Matheson, and Ray Bradbury**, who took notice of **Beaumont** and assisted him. **Beaumont** went on to do numerous Hollywood scripts. Attracting the attention of **Rod Serling** he placed a number of scripts in the first few seasons of the **Twilight Zone**. Perhaps his most notable episode was ***"The Howling Man."***

Later, **Beaumont** worked with **Roger Corman**, adapting in 1963 **Lovecraft's *"The Strange Case of Charles Dexter Ward."*** As **Lovecraft** was barely known, it was pawned off as an **Edgar Allen Poe** story. **Corman** coaxed Vincent Price to star with **Debra Paget**, veterans **Lon Chaney, Jr.** and **Elisha Cook, Jr.**

Ralph Scholl was named President of **Southwest Manuscripters in** 1959. Our guest speakers that year were, **Charles Hillinger & John Perkins, Joe Brennan, Maria Metlova, Robert Kirsh, Marvin Wald, Mark Clifton, Arthur Julian, Bert M. Anderson, Leonard Wibberley, Rod Serling** and **Ray Bradbury** (of course!).

Charles Hillinger

Charles Hillinger began his career at **The Times** in 1946 in the editorial library, soon becoming a general-assignment reporter. He eventually began focusing on feature writing, and wrote nearly 6,000 human-interest stories before retiring from the paper in 1992.

He covered the **Beatles** during their visit to **Los Angeles** in 1964 to perform at the **Hollywood Bowl**. He also was aboard the aircraft carrier **Hornet** in 1969 to report on the historic splash-down in the Pacific of the **Apollo 11** mission-to-the-moon astronauts.

But it's for his stories about people from all walks of life, and their sometimes unusual pursuits, that **Hillinger** is best remembered.

Robert R. Kirsch was a journalist, lecturer and author. He worked as a reporter, feature writer and literary critic for various Southern California newspapers, was a lecturer in journalism at **UCLA**, dean of college at **International Community College**, and a executive story consultant for **Universal Studios.**

In 1960 **Manville Chapman** was elected **President** of the **Manuscripters**. It was our **10th Anniversary**, and we had **Fenton Barnshaw, Ray Bradbury, J.E. Ransom, Chistopher Knopf, Ardythe Hitchcock, Dorothy B. Hughes, Frank Riley, Leonard Freeman, Margaret Leighton** and **Charlotte Armstrong** as guest speakers.

Frank Riley

Frank Riley was the pseudonym of **Frank Rhylick**, an American science fiction author best known for co-writing (with **Mark Clifton**) the novel ***"They'd Rather Be Right,"*** which won a **Hugo Award** for Best Novel during 1955. He was a syndicated travel columnist and editor for the **Los Angeles Times**, and editor of the **Los Angeles Magazine**. He also wrote advertisements for **See's Candies**, screenplays, short fiction such as the ***"Father Anton Dymek"*** mysteries and was a host of a radio program in the **Los Angeles** area.

Loren Roberts was our 1961 **President. Robert Bloch, Arthur Julian, Harry Lewis, Chas Beaumont, Maren Elwood, Ardath Hitchcock, Mark Clifton, Paul Wellman, Ray Bradbury and Charlotte Armstrong** blessed our podium with their presence.

Robert Bloch

Robert Bloch's interest in the fantastic was influenced by his childhood love of the films of **Lon Chaney** and a 1927 of an issue of ***Weird Tales***, a pulp magazine which specialised in macabre and supernatural fiction.

It was by reading ***Weird Tales*** that **Bloch** first discovered the work of **H.P. Lovecraft**, the creator of a series of stories which would become known as the **Cthulhu Mythos**. With the onset of the **Great Depression**, the **Bloch** family moved to Milwaukee, where, in 1933, **Bloch** began a correspondence with **Lovecraft** that would continue until the latter's death in 1937. It was at **Lovecraft's** suggestion that **Bloch** tried his hand at writing short stories. **Bloch's** first professional sale (***"Lilies"*** for ***Marvel Tales***) came in 1934, and his first sale to ***Weird Tales*** (***"The Secret in the Tomb"***) came a few months later.

He worked on a radio show and wrote for a collection of tales with **Henry Kuttner**. In 1959, he published a novel, ***"Psycho,"*** which was later made into a film by **Alfred Hitchcock**.

In the fall of 1959, much to his surprise, **Bloch** won science fiction's prestigious **Hugo Award** for his short story horror fantasy ***"That Hell-Bound Train."***

Over the years **Robert Bloch** has written almost innumerable stories for print and many movie and television scripts.

In 1962 **Dave Bean** was our **President** and **Charles Chapel**, the **Gordons, Jesse Lasky, Frank Rhylick, James H. Moore, Bert Anderson, Charles Beaumont, Mark Clifton, Dorothy B. Hughes, Ray Bradbury** and **Harriet Pratt** were the guests for that year.

The Gordons are crime fiction authors **Gordon Gordon** and his wife **Mildred Gordon**. Both attended the University of Arizona where they met and later married in 1932. They have written many crime fiction novels and screenplays

He was an editor of the **Tucson Citizen** newspaper, was a publicist with **20th Century Fox** from 1935-1942 then served as an **FBI** counter-intelligence agent during **World War II.** She was a teacher, an editor of **Arizona Highways** magazine, worked for **United Press** and wrote ***The Little Man Who Wasn't There.***

Their credits include; ***Experiment in Terror*** with **Lee Remick**, ***That Darn Cat*** for Disney, ***Make Haste to Live, The FBI Story,*** among many others.

As a husband-and-wife team, they jointly won: **1954 Book Society of Great Britain Award, 1965 American Humor Society Award, 1965 Writers Guild of America Award, and 1970 University of Arizona Achievement Award**

In 1963, apparently **Mark Clifton** and **Nyles Walton** shared the Presidency. The **Gordons, Laura Wilck, Daniel Clinton, F.A. Rockwell, Charlotte Armstrong, Fritz Lieber, Meyer Dolinsky (Mike Dolinsky** - of T.V. and Movies), **Charles Hillinger** (Times) and **Steve Gardner** were our speakers plus we had a **Charles Beaumont Panel**.

Fritz Leiber

Perhaps best known for his heroic fantasy work, **Fritz Leiber** also created an exciting range of science fiction that reflected his various enthusiasms, cats, chess and the theater.

Leiber became interested in writing through correspondence with a college friend, with whom he collaborated in 1939 in the creation of the heroic-fantasy duo ***Fafhrd and the Grey Mouser***. The adventures of this pair became central to **Leiber's** career, comprising a lengthy series that includes ***The Swords of Lankhmar*** (1970), arguably the greatest modern heroic-fantasy novel.

Leiber's first important work of science fiction, meanwhile, was ***Gather, Darkness!*** (1950), in which a religious dictatorship is overthrown by rebels who disguise their super-science as witchcraft. In the 1950s, he created the ***Change War*** series. The initial volume, The Big Time (1961), takes place entirely in one room (an R & R location called the Place, sited beyond normal realities); suggestive of a play in prose form, it reflects **Leiber's** background in theater (both his parents were **Shakespearean** actors, and **Leiber** himself acted on both stage and screen, including a small part in the 1936 **Greta Garbo** film ***Camille***).

The Big Time (1961) won a **Hugo** award for Best Novel, as did **Leiber's** most ambitious science fiction work, ***The Wanderer*** (1964) , a long disaster novel telling of the havoc caused by the arrival of a strange planet in the solar system. Its mosaic narrative technique, through which events are observed through a multiplicity of viewpoints, foreshadowed the profusion of similar novels and films in the 1970s. **Leiber** won a further **Hugo** for ***"Ship of Shadows"*** (1969) and completed the double of **Hugo and Nebula** awards for the third time with ***"Catch that Zeppelin!"*** (1975).

Noted also for his fantasies in modern settings, such as ***"Belsen Express"*** (1975), **Leiber** was the most influential model for the sudden creation in the 1980s of the subgenre of contemporary (or urban) fantasy. By refusing to create an easily recognizable template for his science fiction, however, he may have sacrificed some popularity in that genre. In compensation, he was the only writer of his generation developing and producing his best genre work in the late 1970s.

Leiber's many awards include the 1975 **Grand Master of Fantasy (Gandalf) Award**, the 1976 **Life Achievement Lovecraft Award,** the 1981 **Grand Master Nebula,** six **Hugos**, four **Nebulas** and approximately 20 others.

Robert Dreizler presided in 1964 and **Ray Bradbury, Roy Marsh, Mike Rosen, Rosemary de Camp, Charles Hillinger, Rod Serling, E. Joseph Cossman, Jerry Goff, Lillian Baker, Renee Taylor**, the **Gordon's** and **Allen Nixon** joined us.

Rosemary DeCamp

Rosemary DeCamp had been our guest before 1964 in February of 1951. She was an American television and movie actress. She began her career on **radio** in the role of secretary **Judy Price** on the ***"Dr. Christian"*** series in 1937. She made her film debut in ***"Cheers for Miss Bishop"*** and appeared in many **Warner Brothers** films, including ***"Eyes in the Night," "Yankee Doodle Dandy"*** playing **Nellie Cohan** opposite **James Cagney**, and **Nora Prentiss**. She also played the mother of the character played by **Sabu** in ***"Jungle Book."***

DeCamp played **Peg Riley** in the early television sitcom ***"The Life of Riley,"*** was a regular on **NBC**'s ***"The Bob Cummings Show"*** in the 1950s, and played **Marlo Thomas'** mother on **ABC**'s ***"That Girl"*** in the 1960s. In 1962, she appeared as a dishonest Southern belle in the **NBC**

sitcom *"Ensign O'Toole"* with **Dean Jones**. She appeared in the role of **Gertrude Komack** in the episode entitled ***"A Little Anger Is a Good Thing"*** on **ABC**'s medical drama ***"Breaking Point."*** **DeCamp** also appeared as **Aunt Helen** on **CBS**'s ***"Petticoat Junction"*** as a replacement for ailing **Bea Benaderet**. Viewers in the 1960s also knew her from her many appearances in commercials for the laundry product **20 Mule Team Borax**.

Rod Serling was born December 25, 1924,in Syracuse, New York. **Helen Foley**, his schoolteacher, encouraged him in his writing and he always believed he owed his success to her. A teacher in **Twilight Zone: The Movie** (1983) was named **Helen Foley** in her honor.

Serling was interested in radio and writing at an early age. He listened to a variety of radio programs, especially thrillers with a fantasy or horror feel. **Arch Oboler** and **Norman Corwin** were two of his favorite writers. His other influences included **H.G. Wells, Ernest Hemingway**, **Edgar Allen Poe, Edward R Murrow** and **H.P. Lovecraft.**

He was a screenwriter, novelist, television producer, and narrator best known for his live television dramas of the 1950s and his science fiction anthology TV series, ***The Twilight Zone***. **Serling** was active in politics, both on and off the screen and helped form television industry standards.

A former boxer, paratrooper and general all-around angry young man, **Rod Serling** was one of the radical new voices that made the **"Golden Age"** of television. Long before ***"Twilight Zone"*** (1959), he was known for writing such high-quality scripts as ***"Patterns"*** and ***"Requiem for a Heavyweight,"*** both later turned into films. Even ***"Twilight Zone"*** featured forays into controversial grounds like racism, Cold War paranoia and the horrors of war.

Rod Serling

Moving to **California** in 1957 the he continued to write for television, he sought to impart a sense of moral responsibility and artistic integrity to the new generation of television writers. He hired scriptwriters whom he respected (such as **Richard Matheson** and **Charles Beaumont**) and his television and cinematic works have reached cult status-enlivening a new interest in one of the great early writers of American television.

In 1969, **NBC** aired a **Serling**-penned pilot for a new series, ***Night Gallery***. Set in a dimly lit museum that was open after hours, the pilot film featured **Serling** (as on-camera host) playing the part of curator introducing three tales of the macabre, focusing more on gothic horror and the occult than did The ***Twilight Zone***.

Michael York

Serling kept his schedule full. When he wasn't writing, promoting or producing his work, he was often seen speaking on college campuses all over the country. He is considered to be one of the most influential writers in Television History and is credited with creating many storytelling methods still used today.

In 1965 **David Kenney** was our club **President**. Our guest speakers were **Robert Kirsch** of the **LA Times**, **Remi Nadeau, John Pimley, Lee Felton** & **Wayne Allen, Shelton Wile, Col. Walter Cronk, Irwin Zucker** & **Froma Sands, Ray Bradbury, E. Joseph Cossman, Jack Matcha** and **Shelley Lowenkopf**.

Ben Britain took over the Presidency in 1966.

In 1967 **Richard Smith** became **President** of the club. **Jack Burkig, Nancy** & **Benedict Freedman,** The **Gordons**, the **Marquants, Richard Landers, James Warner Beelar, Helen Walters, Judith Ransom Mieler, Ray Bradbury, Norman Allestad, Mladin Zarubesa, Irwin Zucker, Robert Kendall** and **Rabbi Moshe Magael** were our guests that year.

Steve McSweeney was our leader in 1968 with **Audrey Kirks, Toohey** & **Bierman, Helen Rogers, Milton S. Gelman, Ray Bradbury, Ray Banks, Larry L. Meyer, Marguerite McClain, Larry Miller, Annemarie Ewing Towner** and the **Gordons** as our guests.

Since those glorious beginnings the **Southwest Manuscripters** has been fortunate to have many top-notch authors as guest speakers. Many popular fiction and non-fiction writers, agents, and publishers have graced our podium with their presence.

In more recent years, we have been fortunate to have as guests such well known celebrities as **Doug Dutton** of **Dutton's Books**, **Michael York**, **Steven Canell**, **Stephen Smoke**, **Dr. Lawrence J. Peter** and

Steve Allen.

Steve Allen was an American television personality, musician, composer, actor, comedian, and writer. Though he got his start in radio, Allen is best known for his television career. He first gained national attention as a guest host on ***Arthur Godfrey's Talent Scouts***. He graduated to become the first host of **The Tonight Show**, where he was instrumental in innovating the concept of the television talk show. Thereafter, he hosted numerous game and variety shows, including ***The Steve Allen Show***, ***I've Got a Secret***, ***The New Steve Allen Show***, and was a regular panel member on **CBS'** ***What's My Line?*** He also starred in **Universal's** ***The Benny Goodman Story***.

Steve Allen

Allen was a "creditable" pianist,and a prolific composer, having penned over **14,000** songs, one of which was recorded by **Perry Como** and **Margaret Whiting**, others by **Steve Lawrence** and **Eydie Gorme**, **Les Brown**, and **Gloria Lynne**. **Allen** won a **Grammy** award in 1963 for best jazz composition, with his song ***The Gravy Waltz***.

His vast number of songs have never been equaled. **Allen** wrote more than 50 books, has two stars on the **Hollywood Walk of Fame** and a Hollywood theater named in his honor.

Allen's clear and open mind enabled him to move lightly from the most complex subjects to nutty comedy. He used it on a 24-hour-a-day schedule, finding ideas literally while waking and sleeping. Always ready to extract them, **Allen** had small tape-recorders everywhere: in his pockets, in the bathroom, by his bed, in his car. This system supplied the raw material for the numerous **Allen** activities.

By 1956, ***Tonight*** had spawned such future stars as **Steve Lawrence** and **Eydie Gorme** and **Andy Williams**. Among stars who appeared with **Allen** early in their careers are **Louis Nye, Don Knotts, Tom Poston, the Smothers Brothers, Don Adams, Bill Dana, Jim Nabors, Jackie Vernon, Lenny Bruce, Jonathan Winters, Tim Conway, Lou Rawls, Jackie Mason**, and the **Muppets** - the list is almost endless.

Allen's multi-award winning ***"Meeting of Minds"*** series aired on the **PBS Network**. The programs, in talk-show format, featured serious discussions with such guests as **Aristotle, Plato, Socrates, Augustine, Aquinas, Karl Marx, Voltaire, Adam Smith, Florence Nightingale, Elizabeth Barrett Browning, Cleopatra, Marie Antoinette** and other figures from history.

"I'm always busy," he noted, **"but always doing things I enjoy. I rarely occupy myself with things that bug me. I'm very fortunate in that not many of us are allowed to live for kicks and get paid for it."**

As our motto on the front cover proudly states:
"Our aim is to encourage writers to express their talents and develop a unique writing voice by providing a nurturing environment in which to share their gifts."

Through the years our membership has grown to include novelists, screenwriters, poets, writers of children's books, science fiction, non-fiction, journalism, and so many more. We encourage and sponsor workshops and critique groups where budding writers get a chance to have "one-on-one" writing experiences with more seasoned authors.

To help encourage our member writers, our group holds three writing contests a year; Stories, Articles and Poetry.

Winners of these contests not only win a cash prize, but are guaranteed to have their items published in our newsletter, ***The Write Stuff***, if they choose!

At each meeting, members of our practiced group are chosen to read excerpts from their works, as well as at the two yearly parties, where the **Writers' Showcase** features selected readings.

Our club meets every month at a location in the **South Bay** region of **Los Angeles County**. At this time we are meeting in the **Palos Verdes Peninsula Center Library** on Silver Spur Road.

Thank you all! Your President 2012. Ildy Lee
Visit our web site at ***http://www.coliserv.net/swm/*** to find out more about our club and its events.

We are the oldest writer's group in the USA, south of the Rockies, yet we are the most affordable! Join us to get peer support, learn from our expert speakers, win our writing contests, get our newsletter, enjoy our summer and holiday parties and join in the fun! Check out what we do and contact us. (See last page.)

CONTESTS AND AWARDS

SWM Awarded by the city of Torrance

Ray Bradbury and Bernadette Shih

The Shakespeare Poetry Contest winners 2012: Gwen Binegar, Alan Cook and Ildy lee

MaryAnne M. Butterfield is awarding professor Dan Lambert

A selection from Alan Cook's books; our prolific mystery writer.

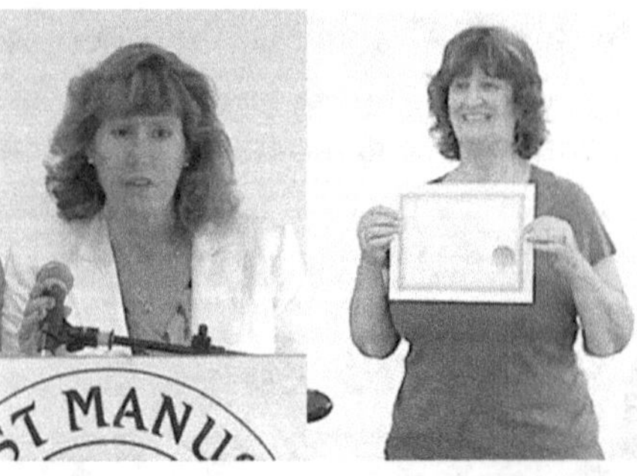

Beth Whittenbury esq. Contest Chair

Judy Sunderland Incoming President 2013

Ildy Lee President 2012

Stephen Smoke Award-winning author

MEETINGS AND SPEAKERS

Author Adam Chester is a riot!

Janis Lukstein and Ildy clown around!

Stan Corwin CEO. Pinnacle Books

Vickey Kalambakal

Bonnie Folkart and Maury Garnholz

Van Gordon Editor/Historian

Sam Weller, Janis, Ray Bradbury, Bernadette, Alan

Stephen Smoke, Bernadette, Ray, Carol

Jeri Fonté

Glenn Willis, Anita Lutt

Lois Hendricks

José Manazia, Ildy (awarded), Dan and MaryAnne

Beverly Knudson and Faith B. Goldman

The SouthWest Manuscripters on TV

Faith and Ildy

Carol Sperling, Treasurer.

Connie Bessaman Natt

William Whittenbury our youngest member

Mary Anne Golden, Ildy Lee, and Dan Lambert

Dan has more than one trick under his sleeves

Ray Bradbury, Ildy Lee and Edith Battles

Carolee Bradshow, writer

Jay Brown, writer for TV
and former President

Richard Bradshow, our newest member, shares his latest books.

Irwin Zucker, CEO, speaker.

Sharon Scott, screenwriter, speaker.

Cathy Gould, speaker

Connie, our new co-treasurer. Dear Paula, we'll miss you! Hey guys, we're in the news!

Austen Pell esq. Past president. Professor Lambert is always wise… Alan Cook speaks.

Austen Pell is thanking Cathy Gould, president of the Palos Verdes library, for graciously housing our club.

Just like Austen, Beth Whittenbury is also a lawyer, and a bestselling author. Wow!

Janis Lukstein's haiku is published in a newspaper.

Judy Sunderland is the incoming president.

Vickey smiles, her latest book is doing great.

Van's dedication to the club is unsurpassed

Lyn Moran, a prominent writer and journalist.

Gwen is a Shakespeare Poetry Award winner

Good bye to our wonderful Richard Meyers.

Hello to fame: Stephen Smoke wrote over 30 books!

PARTY TIME!

After his speech author Adam Chester, who played for Elton John, gave us a concert. We all danced!
SouthWest Manuscripters hosted at Ildy Lee's house an evening of
POETRY and SONGS:

Our Award-winning poets gave a stunning performance

KC Johnson

Alan Cook

Bernadette Shih

Stephen Smoke's poem mesmerized the audience & Niki B.'s award winning photos were amazing.

Stephen and Ildy both songwriters, charmed the audience with songs from their latest albums.

Stephen sang songs from his innovative multi media e-book "Cathedral of the Senses." It's an amazing new concept using cutting-edge technology. Check out his site: www.StephenSmoke.com

Ildy entertained as a French chanteuse, then she surprised her audience as Elvis (below) with a show she wrote about his compelling love story with Priscilla, based on his most famous hit songs.

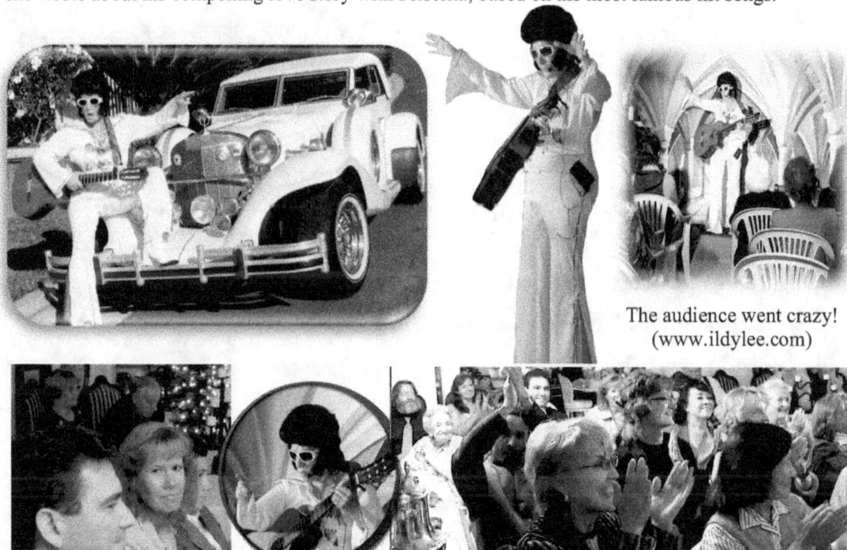

The audience went crazy!
(www.ildylee.com)

JOIN US!
Be part of a reknown writer's club!
WHO? We are the SouthWest Manuscripters,
with over fifty years collection of writers to hobnob and confer with,
including such illuminaries and members as Ray Bradbury.
WHERE? We meet in the Community Room of the Palos Verdes Peninsula Library,
WHEN? usually on third Mondays, starting at 6 p.m.
Sometimes we even serve refreshments. Networking starts at 5:30
WHAT are we doing? Meetings always include a main speaker. Come and learn from successful writers, publishers, or editors. Feel their passion as they speak about their work.. We also share new acceptances for publication, unusual rejections, recognize new members, and enjoy three minute readings of new material by members who wish to do so.
HOW much? Dues run $ 25/yr, and include a monthly newsletter, a summer picnic, and a Christmas party. Only $ 25 a year? It's a bargain!
We hold 3 contests through the year for poetry, short stories, and articles.
Contact info:
Website: http://www.coliserv.net/swm/
E-mail: E-mail: swmtws@hotmail.com
or President Ildy Lee: ildylee@cox.net

www.ingramcontent.com/pod-product-compliance
Lightning Source LLC
Chambersburg PA
CBHW071107250626
47159CB00002B/632

9780989014601